D0359181

LOYALTIES

BY CARL BERNSTEIN

ALL THE PRESIDENT'S MEN *(with Bob Woodward)*
THE FINAL DAYS *(with Bob Woodward)*
LOYALTIES: A SON'S MEMOIR

LOYALTIES
CARL BERNSTEIN

a son's memoir

Tameside Public Libraries

CEN, **995787**

MACMILLAN
LONDON

All of the events in this book are real; the names of a few participants
have been changed.

Copyright © Carl Bernstein 1989

All rights reserved. No reproduction, copy or transmission of this
publication may be made without written permission. No paragraph of
this publication may be reproduced, copied or transmitted save with
written permission or in accordance with the provisions of the
Copyright Act 1956 (as amended). Any person who does any
unauthorised act in relation to this publication may be liable to criminal
prosecution and civil claims for damages.

First published in the United States of America 1989 by
Simon and Schuster, Simon & Schuster Building, Rockefeller Centre,
1230 Avenue of the Americas, New York, New York 10020

First published in the United Kingdom 1990 by
MACMILLAN LONDON LIMITED
4 Little Essex Street London WC2R 3LF
and Basingstoke

Associated companies in Auckland, Delhi, Dublin, Gaborone,
Hamburg, Harare, Hong Kong, Johannesburg, Kuala Lumpur, Lagos,
Manzini, Melbourne, Mexico City, Nairobi, New York, Singapore and
Tokyo

ISBN 0-333-52135-8

A CIP catalogue record for this book is available from the British
Library

Printed in Great Britain by WBC Ltd, Bristol & Maesteg

THIS BOOK IS FOR MY PARENTS.
I AM PROUD OF THE CHOICES THEY MADE.

———

IT IS FOR JACOB AND MAX—THE NEXT GENERATION.
AND IT IS FOR BOB WOODWARD AND KATHLEEN TYNAN.

Laundry (1978)

"At some point you're going to confront your feelings," says my friend. I'm not sure that she comprehends the depth of pain and anger. And about what? Does anyone really care what happened to two or ten or twenty or thirty people who were on the fringes of the failing social and political movements of the last generation?

Yesterday was unbearable. Transcribing pages and pages and pages of notes from a tape recorder, thousands and thousands of words, most of them about the chaos that ruled our house when we were little, the inability of my mother to get a grip on running the household and what seemed like the accompanying abdication of parenthood by my father. I'm not sure that it contributes to an understanding of the times.

Which, after all, was how this got started. The typewriter would deliver of itself a calm, dispassionate account of that last undisturbed corner of our national nightmare. Names, dates, places, transcripts, footnotes, appendices. Scrupulously journalistic. Feelings weren't contemplated.

3

Not for the first time I lost the thread last week. Very depressing. Long walks on the beach with my friend, describing the problem: How do you keep from becoming self-indulgent? Why should the reader be interested in my obsession? How do I deal with my father's resistance and obvious disapproval?

Keep writing, says my friend; his reaction is part of the story. The material will carry you.

The files fill the cottage now. Spiral notebooks from two years of interviewing. Bookshelves overflowing with bound accounts of lives spent in service to the Party, informing on the Party, declaring war on the Party—almost all of it irrelevant. Reams of transcripts—the testimony of my mother, my father, of those who held me and bathed me and taught me. Cassettes, voices from the grave, heaped in boxes—my grandmother, trying to explain away her coolness to my parents' marriage. Clippings from the paper's morgue ("Bernstein, Sylvia, Local Commie," says the file heading on my mother).

His personal files—musty, mildewed—are here, too, and those of the union. For years they were kept under the steps in Silver Spring. It seemed unlikely that the FBI would look there. It also seemed unlikely that the FBI would come to my Bar Mitzvah. But they did.

I cannot remember a single instance of my father complaining, which is not as surprising as it might seem; I have hardly any memory of him raising his voice, whatever the provocation, at either his children or his government. He has always been a man of quiet passion, eloquent and reasoned even in anger, capable perhaps of hate but not of retribution. I must have wished otherwise, for I have long carried this sense, probably exaggerated, of his frailty, have allowed my mind to confuse his gentleness with defenselessness. His physical appearance, particularly to a son who wanted desperately that his father concern himself with something heroic, like

4

football, instead of with matters of the mind, always contributed to this sense: bantam, diminutive, those short arms and spindly legs that I allowed to embarrass me when we went to the beach. Fully dressed, the impression was usually no less helpless, partly because of the indifference with which he clothed himself, but mostly because of the absentmindedness he seemed to carry almost everywhere. I have seen him dry the dinner dishes and then stack them neatly in the refrigerator. It was only when I had reached my thirties and discovered myself similarly afflicted that I began to consider the view of his closest friends that the absentmindedness might be somehow endearing. His obliviousness could be hilarious, his private thoughts so consuming that at times it would not be unreasonable for a stranger to assume that he was conducting some kind of séance with himself. I can remember being awakened some mornings by the sound of talking downstairs, and, tiptoeing down the steps, I would find my father in motion, deep in conversation with himself, dressed in a robe haphazardly tied, a cigar stuck in the corner of his mouth, head cocked to one side, ashes tumbling onto the burgundy robe as he paced the room.

What were his aspirations? I've often wondered since. What are his regrets? He is a man who wanted more than anything else to participate in the events of his day, who came to Washington to be a participant and, by the age of forty, found himself excluded.

Was there some mechanism of self-protection that failed, that became short-circuited by ideological or other currents? Surely by 1942 it was possible to foresee that membership in the Communist Party, if discovered, would be ruinous. Above all my father is a cautious man, a believer in weighing the consequences of behavior before choosing a course, or so he has always seemed to me. With the exception of that decision to join the Communist Party, I do not know of a single act in his adult life that might be characterized as reckless. He is a man who eschews unnecessary danger. He is quite capable of courage, won't be swayed by fashion, refuses to compromise with principle—but all that is something quite apart from consciously reaching a decision bound to cause him so much pain.

What must he have thought when he looked across the witness table at Senator Jim Eastland's fat face, listened to Eastland tell him that he was on the receiving end of an investigation into "treason and a bunch of traitors"? He was already two years out of a job by then, a Columbia Law School graduate learning the laundry business, a Marxist turned reluctant capitalist, proprietor of his share of America, the Georgia Avenue Bendix Automatic Laundry, twenty-six machines filled with the dirty diapers and socks and underwear of poor blacks. I can remember him coming home exhausted each evening, his hands red and swollen from feeding bleach and soap into the tops of the machines, emptying the day's laundry tickets from his pockets onto the dining table and counting the day's washes. For a while I loved the laundry business, thought it was quite glamorous really; spending time in the laundromat was definitely preferable to being in my grandparents' tailor shop on the better side of town. The laundry tickets, with their sequential numbers printed in red, the cotton sacks stamped QUALITY LAUNDRY BAG CO. (another of my father's ventures), the scales in the front window, were symbols of a vocation that I could understand. No more unfathomable talk about union organizing. Even a child could understand about "washes," could comprehend that two hundred loads of laundry on a Saturday was a good day. Even a child's friends could understand, especially friends from the shule, because their fathers too were in the laundry business.

If ever some historian of laundry chronicles the trade in a definitive manner, it will be dutifully recorded that in Washington, D.C., in the early 1950s the neighborhood laundry business turned left. I don't know who was the first to try it, but word spread quickly that a living could be made—if just barely—in laundry. Everyone had his own turf, and I think there must have been a gentleman's agreement, just like in the Mafia, about territory: Dad worked the Griffith Stadium area, Mike Samols had Congress Heights, Leon Malkin was in Mount Pleasant, Iz Paskoff was in Dupont Circle, and Bill Hayes was in Georgetown. (As the choice of locations would indicate, Bill was the only one to become a truly successful merchant;

6

when times got better and jobs were to be had in accounting and fund-raising, Bill stayed in Georgetown, where he and his wife opened a Mexican craft shop that did very well.)

I'm not exactly sure when the notion of my father being "different" from other fathers began to tug so strongly, but the sense of shame, of being threatened, of being vulnerable to something over which I had no control, came early. Sometimes I hated him for it, and I articulated my rage through whatever misdemeanor was closest at hand: smashing to bits those 78-rpm Asch recordings of Woody Guthrie and Leadbelly and the Almanac Singers, going to 8 A.M. Mass with the kids from St. Ann's, rejoining them in the afternoon to try out for the Catholic Youth Organization football team, stuffing my pockets full of malted-milk balls from the Sears candy counter. The purposefulness of some of these episodes never occurred to me or my parents, who, as I recall, attributed most of the difficulties to nothing more dialectical than the pernicious influence of my friend Johnny Gianaris.

I can remember trying to confront the source of the family's un-spoken troubles only once with my father, after he had been hauled before the Eastland committee in the Senate—I'm not exactly sure how long after, maybe a few weeks, maybe it was even months. We were riding in the car, just the two of us in the family's beat-up '47 Plymouth, and I came right out and asked the question, with even fewer formalities than the Senator had seen fit to observe. "Dad, are you a Communist?" Just like that.

More than anything I remember the silence that followed and my not daring to look at him, staring instead at the green metal dash, waiting, hoping. I suppose the silence told me more than the answer that finally followed, was more definitive, but I was hardly listening anyway by that time: I was aware at last how much my question had hurt him. I had no sense then, of course, that the child's question was far tougher than the Senator's. In answering Eastland he could at least maintain some semblance of dignity, honor, principle. My question offered no escape; there is no Fifth Amendment for eight-year-olds. Surely he knew this. The answer I wanted was no, and I like to think now that he tried to give it to me. The temptation to lie must have been great, but it was too late and he knew it. There was nothing left to do but dissemble. Yes, he had been accused of being a Communist, by a man who had no real way of knowing whether he was a Democrat, a Republican, or a Communist. The man was a well-known liar and these were bad times—charges were flying everywhere, outrageous charges, unfair charges. Many friends of the family had also been accused, and there was no truth to most of what people were saying or what the newspapers were reporting. The fact was that he and Mom and their friends were *progressive* people who were being smeared because of what they believed in —not because they were members of the Communist Party.

I didn't ask any questions when he finished explaining, and I'm sure he guessed that my silence meant that I knew. It took twenty-five years before I asked him that question again. When we got home and out of the car on that afternoon in 1952, he put his arm around me and held me close to him as we walked toward the house. At that moment, perhaps for the first time, I felt protective toward him.

There are times when I am genuinely enthusiastic about this inquiry into the past. Such moments tend to occur when I describe in just-the-facts-ma'am fashion what it is that I'm working on: "An account of the witch-hunts leading up to the McCarthy era and what happened to a small group of people who were in Washington at the time, and then what happened to their children. Two generations."

The degree of straightforwardness depends, of course, on whom I'm talking to. I tell some people (usually those who have some idea of the facts anyhow) that at least part of the narrative will be "personal," whatever that means. Sometimes I add that my father acted as defense counsel in a number of loyalty cases and that his old files are the starting point for my inquiry. That is usually enough to satisfy those who might have heard vaguely about the family background. As often as not, people interrupt at this point to talk about someone they went to college with who was either the son or daughter or cousin of one of the Hollywood Ten. And I, without having uttered an untrue word, am in the clear.

Then there is a tiny group, my closest friends really, with whom I'm much more open about the family's history and my attempt to make some sense of it. They are all very encouraging. Even from them, however, I find myself withholding. The whole Communist Party question is usually skirted. Somehow that stigma remains: today it is honorable and, in some circles, even heroic to have been on the left in the perilous epoch just past; but respectability and rehabilitation have rarely been accorded those known to have been actual members of the Party. The true romance of American Communism may be the widely held belief that the Party was fundamentally an organization to which thousands of people were falsely accused of belonging.

Not surprisingly, I have been less than straightforward at times with members of my family about aspects of what I'm doing. My mother, especially, is mortified about the whole thing and becomes more so with every new indication that there might be a book about them. She phoned one day to ask me, rather incoherently, what plans she and Dad should be making about life insurance. At least I think that was what she was asking; there was so much circumnavigation around the subject that it was hard to tell. First she inquired awkwardly about my trip to the Coast—was the weather nice, did I have fun, was it interesting, how many hours did I spend with the Gellers? ("Twenty hours on tape, oh my God.") When I hung up the phone I said to my wife, "I think my mother would like me to believe that this project is killing her."

Two days later she called again. "Did you ever sign the contract for the book?" she asked.

I reminded her that I'd already told her the contract was completed.

"No, I mean have you actually signed it—formally."

Weeks ago, I repeated.

"That's not what you said. Your father and I were discussing it last night. You said that everything had been put together, that there was an agreement but you hadn't actually signed it."

"Too late," I interrupted; the contract was signed. She should relax, trust me, reconcile herself.

"It's hard for me to relax about. I've never been happy about it, I get so upset about it—it's something that always upsets me." This said with surprising calm.

"You know," she told me at dinner on her sixty-second birthday, in 1977, "one of the joys of the past few years has been the feeling that all that is behind us, that *the troubles* are over. Even the FBI doesn't seem to care much anymore—they hardly ever come around to check on where your father is working." For the first time their lives are not defined by political considerations. Their friend Mark Geller made an observation bearing on this: "I have a sense of your folks, especially Sylvia, being part of the neighborhood in a way that they never were. They're not outsiders anymore. She runs next door for this or that, a neighbor brings over a pie when she hears that you kids are coming to dinner . . ." There's no more of the old kind of subterfuge, no more living like fugitives. Mom goes to work every day and sells Boehm porcelain birds at the department store, Dad gets on the plane to raise money so the National Conference of Christians and Jews can carry on its good works, none of their children is in trouble with the law . . . So it is neither unreasonable nor surprising that they don't wish to see their idyll disturbed. And by me, of all people, not some G-man in a snap-brim hat.

My father's attitude is only a little more accepting than my mother's. I first broached the subject in 1975. I wanted to take a leave of absence from the paper, I told him, and try writing a long piece about Truman's loyalty purges. Maybe include some stuff about the union.

Eyebrows raised, distress signals.

Hadn't he been saying for years that maybe someday he'd try a book on the subject, that it was one of the reasons he'd saved all the

10

old files? Hadn't he once suggested that we do it together? This was when I was still a teenager, right after I'd first gone to work.

Now, though, he urged me to stay at the paper. The advice was not unexpected

And just as predictably I rejected it. There is a long, rather consistent history to this business of how I seek advice and counsel from my father.

In the abstract I've always valued his judgment more highly than anyone else's, especially on questions that might be regarded as either moral or political. He has an innate sense of decency that leads him almost unerringly to the proper course, the correct conclusion. He seems never to get weighed down by the excessive ideological baggage that burdens so many of his comrades; nor does his mind become clouded by whatever trendy ephemera might be mesmerizing the media on the major questions of the day. He arrives at his judgments carefully, yet almost effortlessly, bringing pragmatism to a wellspring of what, in another age, might have been termed humanism, in the best sense of that overworked and misused word. I, of course, experience great difficulty in deciding where I stand on even some of the most elemental questions of the day. It's my reportorial training—the result of forever finding reasons to render complicated what should be simple judgments, tossing opposing facts into the air like so many apples and oranges. For years I have relied on my father to lead me out of these intellectual and ethical thickets. But there is another side to this equation: On those questions that have concerned the major decisions of my life —personal, professional—I have almost unfailingly followed my own instincts, reached judgments independent of his advice. Skipping college, leaving the *Washington Star* at age twenty to apprentice with a favorite editor in the swamp of Jersey journalism, getting married—those were not occasions on which I sought his advice. On the rare occasions when I have gone to him on the verge of a major decision, it has been as a courtesy, as part of some ritual observed between father and son. Respect is conveyed. But little else. I might give him the illusion perhaps of his participating in this

11

decision or that—let him know what I am thinking and then hear out his response. But the fact is that, ultimately, I don't trust him on the big questions.

Since that meeting when I first raised the subject, my father has gradually become more resigned to the project. There was a respite when I went back to the paper for a few months, but I don't think he was at all surprised when I left for good; I didn't even call to say I was thinking of doing it. Instead I phoned afterward. I reached my mother. "I've quit," I said. "To do the project."

"Don't you think you should have discussed it with us first?" I was thirty-three at the time.

"Nope," I said.

Several weeks later I began interviewing my father. The first session turned immediately into a wrestling match over the Communist Party question. My plan had been to avoid the whole subject for a while. There was so much to learn about his life—his boyhood, his parents, the college years, the early days in Washington. I would cover that ground first and sneak up on the later years.

Did he ever think about his childhood? I asked.

He seemed surprised by the question and shifted in his seat. "Uh, no." His mind was elsewhere. Something fundamental had to be understood before we went further. He wouldn't discuss anything having to do with the Communist Party. "That's why I pleaded the Fifth Amendment. It's key, really key. It's a private thing. I took a principled position on it many years ago, and I maintain it. It's nothing for public discussion."

The Party, he stated, was not a major factor in what had happened, anyhow—to him, the union, or the country. "It was never the keystone"—only a smokescreen.

That was one of the things I wanted to find out, I said. If his assessment was correct, the Communist Party would figure very little in what I wrote. But I had no information, had done very little research, was just beginning to interview.

"People won't talk about it—at least not *our* people, all of whom are still working."

12

I doubted that and said so.

"Maybe Decca," he said, referring to his old friend the writer Jessica Mitford. "But nobody else."

He seemed exasperated at having to explain something so basic. "You take the Fifth Amendment to protect your friends." You couldn't put yourself in a position of jeopardizing others; self-protection was really secondary. Or so he seemed to be saying. "I've never discussed the question with people whom I've made assumptions about. It's a personal thing and it can't be part of your book." Period.

I found myself summoning old reportorial reflexes. I suggested we defer the question for a while, tried to soothe him, assured him he would have a say in however any information from him about the Party would be used. Names could be changed, identifying circumstances altered, people protected.

"Look," he snapped, "you've read Lillian Hellman's book. She skirts these questions very neatly. She's too sharp to leave herself open to that kind of embarrassment." He was talking about *Scoundrel Time*, in which Hellman does not state whether or not she had been a member of the Communist Party. She invoked the Fifth Amendment when asked the question by the House Committee on Un-American Activities in 1952—the occasion of her memorable statement "I cannot and will not cut my conscience to fit this year's fashions." (A more recent biography, by Carl Rollyson, revealed that an early draft of that statement contained an acknowledgment of her having been in the Party from 1938 to 1940.)

The thought crossed my mind that my father must be horrified at the prospect of my running around the country asking old friends about the Party and what they did in their cells and God only knows what else: the son loose in the land as Red-hunting wolf in lamb's disguise.

"You'll never convince me," he continued. "It was a secret organization at the start, and it wasn't the keystone of my life. And I don't have to get involved with it now because I went to a couple of meetings. That's not the important thing. If you want to talk about how I got into the left-wing movement, and got involved in the labor movement, that's another question. It wasn't the keystone of anything," he repeated.

I argued. It must have been the keystone of something if the mere suggestion of Communist Party membership had caused thousands of people to lose their jobs, be put under surveillance, dragged before committees of Congress.

"Communist Party affiliation really doesn't come into it directly. You have to read the Truman Loyalty Order, which started it all. It's a wide thing. You didn't have to be a member of the Communist Party to be involved in it, to be caught by the order. You weren't accused of actual membership. You were accused of relationships. There were very few cases that I can recall where the issue was whether the guy was really a member of the Communist Party. This was a different kind of business."

And with that his tone changed, the voice softened, became familiar again. "I've been trying to do some preparation, just in my own mind, just to remember how things started. I think if I was writing this . . ."

And I jotted in my notes: "He's got this all worked out—how to structure the book, etc.—to get around The Question."

And he moved smartly into an account of the origins of the Cold War—and its impact on the 1946 convention of the United Public Workers of America. But I'll get to that later.

Book One

Chapter 1

My grandmother's funeral. Curious that she should pick the Bicentennial weekend to leave this world. My father stands a few feet in front of her grave, looking from face to face as he searches for the right word to describe his mother-in-law. She was a *progressive* woman, he says finally and takes a step backward. Oh Christ, I whisper to my sister, he's going to fall into the goddamn grave. There is still a space of three feet between his heel and the edge, but he is lost in his thoughts, his face creased by some memory that he is struggling to articulate. His eyes stop on my cousin Bea, and he takes another step backward. My sister's expression is pleading, prayerful: maybe one of us should step out of the circle and take his arm gently and lead him—like a blind man. Why can't he ever get it all together? Either he's spilling cigar ashes all over himself or his fly is half zipped or he's got the wrong button of his jacket buttoned . . . Jesus. I shut my eyes as he starts to take another step back. When I hear the sureness in his voice I realize that some internal gyroscope has saved him; only then do I allow myself to peek. He is still looking straight ahead at Bea. "She kept this family together," he says of my maternal grandmother. "When her niece needed a place to live, she sheltered her and cooked for her and cared for her as if she was her own daughter. Her house was where everybody ran when there was trouble. She was the glue in this family."

And his hands go into his pockets and at last his eyes leave Bea and he walks absently in a small circle, his cheek trembling a little as he looks upward and contemplates the thought. The moment is so stunning, the cut so swift that in the same instant that I feel the tears rush I can also feel the breath leave my chest. Finally he has shown some anger, indulged himself some bitterness, uncovered himself just enough to display the bruises. It occurs to me how much he must love my mother, how sometimes there is so much gentleness there, such caring between them.

Bea's teeth are slightly bucked, I notice. I hadn't remembered that. As girls she and my mother were both said to be beauties. The years have been kinder to Mom. The last time I saw Bea was on my ninth birthday. She took her daughter Nancy and me to the RKO Keith's to see *High Noon*. Later I was told that Nancy had moved from Washington. But I saw her one afternoon when I was riding my bike. She said her father had told her that he could get into trouble if our families saw each other. He worked at the Capitol, for Senator Humphrey. Years afterward I read in the paper that Nancy's father was under investigation for failing to register as a sugar lobbyist for the Dominican Republic. He and Bea were divorced not long after that, my mother told me.

"Oh yes," says Bea's expression when our glances meet, "your grandmother was such a kind woman." My father's words seem to have been lost on her. There is no comprehension of her transgression, no sense of the hurt to my mother.

When my grandmother's brother went into the hospital, my father is saying (he is polite enough not to mention that it was the loony bin), *she* was the one who visited him every day, brought him food, saw that his affairs were kept in order . . . I look at another of my grandmother's brothers, Uncle Morris with the Florida tan; Uncle

18

Morris who never showed up to visit his brother in the hospital—though he did pay most of the bills. *He* comprehends. I like this unexpected flash of bitterness, I realize—come on, Pop, zing another one in there—it takes my mind off my grandmother. Get a haircut, she said; those were her last words to me.

Uncle Morris is taking quite a beating today. At the funeral home Aunt Rose, my grandmother's sister, started screaming at him, so loud the *Shabbes goy* came running into the room to see whether somebody needed a doctor. *"Vertlozer bruder,"* she wailed. Worthless brother. She chased him into the hall, said he had no business being in the same room as the family. I was outside in the parking lot, reading over my eulogy notes. My father came out and told me. When he finds something funny he gets this wonderful twinkle. He put his arm around me and started wheezing with laughter. Neither of us knew about this particular sibling dispute. Apparently some fifty years earlier Morris and my Uncle Itzel—Rose's husband—had been partners in the delicatessen where my great-grandmother cooked; each of them had put up three hundred dollars to expand the business. Itzel lasted about six weeks before he gave it up to promote socialism and work for the *Jewish Daily Forward*. But Morris never gave Itzel back the three hundred dollars—even, as Aunt Rose says, after the delicatessen became the liquor store and Morris became a millionaire.

At the funeral home, Itzel was the first speaker. He insisted on walking to the podium by himself. Little baby steps. Then he hung his cane on the lectern and began speaking in Yiddish. What a dignity my Uncle Itzel has, what sweetness! I remember, can still feel, his cheek rub across my face, all sandpapery: Keys, keys, keys, he would sing, and dangle a ring full of keys in front of me. My giggling wouldn't stop until my hands closed over them and stopped the jangling. Now he's so frail. When my grandmother died, I went from the hospital to their apartment to tell them. Rose shrieked. Itzel gave a single tiny sob. I went over to his chair and put my arms around him and cried.

My grandmother, his sister-in-law, lived a purposeful life, he says now. She believed in socialism, worked Sundays in the rummage, was president of her Emma Lazarus Club, marched on the Monument with Martin Luther King. (Why doesn't he say something about her cooking? That was *real* purpose.) There was more of her head in that march than her heart, I suspect. Even in the hospital she was talking about the *shvartzes* and giving me a lot of crap about the neighborhood. "When we closed the shop it was already bad. How can you let your wife live in that neighborhood? You could afford Georgetown."

The fact is, of course, that I live in the neighborhood largely because of my grandmother. My mother was born around the corner. From my living-room window I can see the apartment where we all lived before my father came back from the war. The tailor shop was across the street. The first time I went inside the Ontario, with its iron grillwork and marble columns, I must have been about three. My grandfather took me with him to an apartment on the top floor to deliver Judge Edgerton's cleaning. I never forgot the view. I look out those windows now; nothing seems to have changed. The park is timeless. But my grandmother wasn't altogether wrong about the streets.

Her lateness in coming to racial equality, if she really got there at all, infuriated my father. And his priorities infuriated her. "Why is it that for the colored you'll go on strike but for Jewish people you won't go to the corner?" she once asked him. I particularly remember one afternoon in the shop when I reached into the cleaning pile and put on old Whitehead's cap; he was the elevator operator. She lunged from her sewing machine, parting a sea of garments that hung from the hot-water pipes, screaming, "It's the *shvartzer's* hat," and tore it from my head. I tried to grab it back. My grandfather screamed at her through the steam from the presser. She screamed back. Characteristically, she prevailed.

But not with my father. She had wanted her daughter to marry someone who would make money, command respect—a doctor, a practicing lawyer, a dentist even—flesh-and-blood evidence that her struggle had been worth it. Selflessness rewarded, suffering compensated. It was not part of her plan that her only surviving child, secretary-treasurer of the Young Democrats of the District of Columbia, would fall in love with someone with equal disregard for the excellence of his mother-in-law's cooking and the importance of taking his bar exam. He had graduated from law school, and then decided against practicing law. He was daring, radical, oblivious.

Which held a certain attraction for my mother.

A measured coolness persisted; for the rest of my grandmother's life he never referred to her by her name, only by her relationship to the person he was addressing: your mother, your grandmother, your sister, etc. Still, he admired her enormous strength. He came to accept the inevitability of her incessant admonition and implicit criticism. And she grudgingly came to accept the essential rightness of his decisions. He made her laugh and educated her. And in the end he made some kind of final peace with her, loved her even. He came to understand her, I suspect, better than any of us did. He discovered the craft and cunning behind all that chopping and grating—"the certain genius of her latke parties," as he put it during his precarious march around her grave. For days she'd be on the phone to her brothers and sisters and their children, lining them up, making sure that this one or that had a ride, bringing them together by sheer force of will. "Hers was the one house in which we were all truly together," he said, his eyes swollen, his cheeks wet.

How interesting, I thought, that he would so appreciate the concept of family.

His own grandmother died on the Sunday of the Cleveland–Boston Braves World Series. That's how he dates most things: baseball games, horse races, championship fights. But never football, though he watches a good deal of it on television. I think the only game he ever went to was with me, the Redskins and the Giants in 1955. We did a lot of fighting before he relented. At halftime they played "Dixie." He said he would never go again until they integrated the team.

21

He remembers Larry Doby hitting a home run in the '48 Series, but he cannot remember his grandmother's first name. He says I knew her but I have no recollection of it. According to his cousin Maurice in Santa Barbara, she was Rachel Schrier Bernstein and she was born in New York in 1856.

On his mother's side are Czechs—Bohemian Jews who came to this country around the time of the Civil War. His mother and George Jessel's mother were first cousins. Every time my other grandmother—my mother's mother—saw Jessel on television she would telephone. "Turn on Channel Four, your cousin is on," she would say. It made no difference to her that the man's mind was bent and that none of us, save my father, had ever set foot in the same room with him. My maternal grandmother persevered in her belief that there was something aristocratic about my father's past; such invention eased her disappointment about his more immediate circumstances. His background was in fact quite different from my mother's: Both his parents had been born on the East Side of New York; they were second-generation Americans; they spoke English, not Yiddish. They raised their son in a succession of respectable neighborhoods, a little better each time, always comfortable, always a safe step ahead of the blacks.

There had even been some real money in the family. A great-uncle had started out making Turkish cigarettes in a little shop in Manhattan; he hit on the idea of giving premiums—coupons. His outfit, Afternoon Cigarettes, eventually was absorbed by the American Tobacco Company. His desk is in the bedroom in Silver Spring, a beautiful burled-maple rolltop with finely turned Louis XVI legs and a gold-tooled leather writing surface—quite an incongruous piece amid the trappings of a low-ceilinged suburban house of the mid-1950s. It was a wonderful plaything. Dozens of drawers and compartments and letter slots where a child might find some secret cache where Uncle had hoarded a few of his millions, left some hidden legacy for his descendants. On its top are two small color-tinted photographs of my father's parents, framed in silver and bordered with creme oval matting, taken for their forty-fifth anniver-

22

sary. There is just a hint of stoutness in her face—and a shy expression, which is how I remember her: retiring, tender, deferential to my grandfather. He is holding a straw hat, the gleam of a gold cufflink barely visible at the wrist. His necktie, perfectly tied in a small knot, matches the swirled pattern of the handkerchief in the breast pocket of his powder-blue jacket. The overall impression is quite jaunty. In his day he probably would have been called a dandy. I remember his shoes—white, with brown wing tips. He would come to Washington often when I was little and bring me chewing gum, the penny kind, a big round box of it with a hole in the middle. Sometimes I would go on the train to New York with my mother to visit them. Broadway, uptown in the 80s or 90s, a big white stone building with a cobblestone driveway. There was a radio in the living room, on a radiator. He would listen to the news and try to explain about my daddy being away and the war. He died in 1947, six months after my grandmother. I have his obit, from *Women's Wear Daily:* he was a well-known character on Seventh Avenue. He'd started as an errand boy in the cloak-and-suit industry. By the time my father was born, in 1910, my grandfather was one of three partners in the Klein Embroidery Company. The business prospered. They made flags in an era when almost everybody had a flag in the window.

My grandfather ran with a fast crowd—"sporty guys," my father calls them. They went to good restaurants, hung out at the Democratic club, spent freely, gambled. The *Morning Telegraph* was in the house every day, and on days when my grandfather didn't go to the track he placed his bets with bookies. He also enjoyed social pinochle and backroom poker.

Neither of my father's parents read books. Occasionally my grandmother would suggest that my grandfather spend a little less time out with the boys, but he was reasonably attentive and she was uncomplaining. Once they went to Asbury Park; it was their only vacation. My father remembers her as very short and stout and very good-natured and very kind. He started rubbing his eyes when he began talking about her, and his voice got a bit shaky.

My father continues to dope the horses every day, though he wouldn't be caught dead playing pinochle. After all their years together, my mother is the better poker player of the two. She plays every Thursday in a game that remained under FBI surveillance until 1968. I know this because it's in Herb Ratner's file. "Subjects met at the usual hour at the home of Martin Moffatt," it says.

Chapter 2

There is a certain logic—a consistency of temperament and intellect
—that guides my father's politics. It is my mother who is the mystery to me: she, much more than he, values comfort, safety, security. Yet she always seemed to me the more militant, the more
active. The notion of my father at the barricades is unlikely. I was
with *her* when we ran in panic from the charge of the Park Police
cavalry during the battle to integrate the swimming pools; with her
at the Washington lunch counter sit-ins; with her in the offices of
the Defense Committee on the night the Rosenbergs were executed. And it was her appearance before a congressional committee,
three years after my father and Senator Eastland exchanged words,
that in my mind marked us as a family, isolated us, endangered us.

She was called to testify before the House Committee on Un-
American Activities on July 14, 1954. The next day her picture
appeared on the front page of the *Washington Daily News*—arm
upraised, being sworn. "D.C. Housewife Takes Fifth," said the
caption.

Sylvia Bernstein was a member of the white collar section of the Communist Political Association and when her husband returned from the service, she was transferred to the underground club of the Communist Party.

That was the basic allegation, read to her by the chief counsel from an informer's testimony. The story on page one of the next morning's *Washington Post* described my mother and ten other witnesses as "stubborn" and quoted the chairman as saying that their appearance had convinced him "there is a hard core of the Communist Party operating in the Nation's Capital."

My mother does not look stubborn in the picture in the *Daily News*. Scared would be more like it—and stylish, even in one of the severely tailored suits of the period. She remembers putting on a red hat and white gloves that morning. And that afternoon, much more than being frightened, being humiliated—"because the committee knew you were going to take the Fifth and they asked you one question after another for the sake of repetition."

Above my typewriter in Washington is a picture of the two of us, from the *Washington Post*, a clipping from the files, dated June 1944. I found it the first week I went to work there—I was curious and looked up my parents in the paper's library.

VICTORY BABY OF THE WEEK

Carl Milton Bernstein was born three months before his father, Pvt. Alfred Bernstein, went overseas, but Uncle Sam never gave the leave necessary to allow the two to meet. Today, Father's Day, is Carl's parents' fifth wedding anniversary. He and his mother are living at 1601 Argonne Pl. N.W., with her parents, Mr. and Mrs. Thomas Walker. Just before embarking, Pvt. Bernstein wrote his family not to feel badly about his leaving. He said there was a job to be done if they were to lead the kind of life they wanted. Formerly attached to the Senate Committee investigating railroads here, Bernstein was supervising investigator for the West Coast of the Office of Price Administration at the time of his induction.

There is a beautiful softness to the way my mother looks in that picture—remarkably like she looks today, I realize. I am snuggled against her, her left arm around my left side, her right hand cradling my legs. I can remember lying in my bed on Argonne Place and looking into her eyes, the pleasure dancing in them.

I am always theorizing about her, looking for logical explanations, seeking rational answers to questions about feelings. I missed her a lot when I was little, even when she was there, because I was terrified I'd lose her. My sense of her has always been distorted by fear that people were trying to take her away: father, sisters, grand-parents, police, FBI men, members of Congress.

My basic sense of her is lonely. Her easy laughter and nimble conversation disguise some unspoken sorrow, or perhaps that is a projection on my part, the sorrow mine because she and I have never been able to reach any real kind of accord with each other. We walk around it, talk around it, cagily, defensively, each taking refuge in some reservoir of hurt that makes resolution difficult.

I forget sometimes about the qualities that have always drawn my friends to her: the charm, the warmth, her good nature, her empa-thy. Long ago I asked her how she became involved in the move-ment to desegregate the lunch counters. The simplicity of her answer was striking: "I was in Murphy's five-and-dime one day and I saw a Negro woman who was very pregnant and she had another little baby with her. And she had to eat standing up. I never forgot it." Her feel is for people, much more than for books and abstract ideas. She is not an intellectual.

Yet she is capable of considerable detachment and introspection, can summon a self-deprecating humor that lends her a perspective that my father sometimes lacks. "Mostly it was boring," she says of her experience in the Communist Party. "My clearest memory is of interminable talk." Once she was assigned to go into a working-class neighborhood in San Francisco and sell copies of Earl Browder's autobiography; this was during the period before the war when Browder and the Party elders were advocating a no-strike policy in the trade-union movement. "I remember going up on De Haro

Street and trying to sell the book to some guys from the docks, and thinking 'No strikes'? *Men darf meshugge zein*—you have to be crazy."

Much more than my father, she has a sense of place. The house in Silver Spring is very much hers: pretty, informal, neat, inviting, cheerful. She has always striven for an orderliness in her life, and to a remarkable degree has achieved it finally. She works at relationships more than my father; friendships come easily; she nurtures them. She has managed to separate into fairly neat compartments family friends, political friends, neighborhood friends, and professional friends. It was not always that way, of course. Rejection figures large in her scheme of things, and there are scars from that whole middle period of her life—the years of isolation and frustration when she struggled to hold things together. She showed her hurt precisely because she is a person who operates on the basis of what she feels. She had fewer defenses than my father, only her instincts to protect her. When she was approached on the street by an FBI man and asked whether she was ready to become an informer, she was with my sister Mary, then five. She put her arms around my sister and told the man to get away right now, that he was *indecent*.

My mother's Jewish name is Chaih Sura, which Dr. Sachs translated as Idey Silvey when he filled out her birth certificate in 1915, thus beginning a confusion that has caused the bureaucracy considerable difficulty. My grandmother could neither read nor write English well; when she enrolled my mother in school the registrar took down the name as Irene Sylvia Walker. The FBI's report of the poker game identifies my mother as "Sylvia Walker Bernstein, nee Irene Sylvia Walker with aliases Silvey Ida Walker and Silvey Bernstein."

My mother has always called herself Sylvia, though my grandmother called her Silvey.

Her earliest memories are of the neighborhood. She was born at 1809 Eighteenth Street, across from where the Exxon station is now, down the street from Cousin Nathan's tailor shop, the premises of which more recently became the Stoned Soup Food Co-op. Sometimes she has trouble remembering which events in her life occurred during the occupancy of which house, because each so resembled the previous one. Most were on Eighteenth Street or Columbia Road, broad boulevards lined on both sides in those days by the grand apartment houses of the rich and the overcrowded rooming houses of the shopkeepers. Her family always lived directly above the shop, on the second floor. The kitchen was the biggest room in the house, and there was a dining room with a Morris chair in the corner. My mother, her sister Ruth and my grandparents all slept in the same bedroom, overlooking the street. There was never a living room. The bath was on the third floor, where the tenants lived: invariably Gentile, usually immigrant Italians—"the Catholic ladies," my grandmother called them, regardless of whether they had husbands and children. Mrs. Dispencia—her favorite neighbor— made pasta by hand, hung it on the clothesline to dry and earned my grandmother's eternal gratitude by teaching her to make fried breaded tomatoes.

My grandfather, Thomas Walker, was everything that my maternal grandmother was not: carefree, charming, warm, impetuous. He loved books and music and whiskey, all of which she regarded as further evidence of his indolence.

When I was little he'd sit across from me at their kitchen table and pour himself a glass of schnapps. Always just one. "Don't tell your grandmother," he'd say and drink it neat. Then we'd listen on the radio to the Jewish Hour with Max Resnick or to the Met, the Saturday matinee. Popsie (from my first efforts at saying "Grandpa") knew all the operas. He'd tell the stories, much more fun in his version than the dry expositions of Milton Cross. *Rigoletto* was his favorite.

My grandmother tried to throw away his books. He hid them everywhere, stashed them in closets beneath piles of cuttings and trimmings, in bureau drawers way down at the bottom with the whiskey. Later he hid dirty pictures there, too, but I didn't mention that when Mom recalled the business of the books. The pictures weren't exactly porn: nude ladies posed almost demurely—old-fashioned French postcards, I suppose they were. Popsie's bureau drawers were like some splendid bazaar, full of the only tangible wealth of a lifetime of hemming and cuffing and pressing and cleaning. There were dozens of fancy linen handkerchiefs and ivory penknives and lighters and cigarette cases, all gleaming brass and silver and gold, all of it left in the pockets of the capital's gentry and returned unsorted by the cleaning plant. Popsie smoked Old Golds, laid out perfectly in his favorite case, a flat Tiffany silver number with the initials of somebody else whose last name began with W. I have the case now, and his pocket watch, his wedding ring, his thimble and tape measure.

His books—the ones bought after the marriage became less volatile and he and my grandmother had fashioned an uneasy coexistence—are in Silver Spring. They take up a whole corner of the study, volumes bound plainly in pastel buckram, beautiful in their simplicity, the familiar names disguised on their spines in Hebraic script: Shakespeare, Gogol, Peretz, Aleichem, Shelley, Turgenev, Dreiser, Hemingway, Molière, Goethe . . .

He would take me with him to the Jewish bookstore on Kennedy Street on Sundays and buy a book—each week a single volume, poetry as often as prose—and the *Freiheit*, the Yiddish Communist daily. Until the day he died in 1967 he had no use for the *Forward* —or the Socialists. *"Fareters,"* traitors of the cause, he called them, and he didn't much like having any of them into his house—except, of course, for Uncle Itzel, his brother-in-law.

My mother's happiest memories of her childhood are of parties around my grandmother's table: singing and talking and eating and drinking. Her parents and their friends were a very gay group of young people then—full of hope about the new land, about the old land and its new order. Here the work was grueling, the hours exhausting, the pay insulting, but the Cossacks and pogroms were behind, and ahead lay socialism—for Russia, for Europe, for America. In the evenings and on weekends they would gather and celebrate one another. There would be Yiddish songs and long political

30

discussions and recitations of poetry and stories of escape and letters from home. Schnapps would be poured and there would be a thick cherry jam that you'd put into tea in the winter and into seltzer in the summer. And pickled watermelon that came from a brine-filled barrel, and my grandmother's potato latkes.

My mother produces a picture from a box. They are all so young: my grandfather rakish, Itzel frail even in his twenties, Aunt Rose so soft and pretty in sepia, my grandmother looking relaxed in a way I never saw her. My mother identifies the others: Berkowitz the jeweler and his wife, an actress in the Yiddish theater, "D'Actrisse" they called her. Joe Rinis the carpenter, who testified before the Un-American Committee not long before my mother; Dr. Sachs the obstetrician; Dave Efros the house painter, whose widow, Anne, now lives at the Hebrew Home with Rose and Itzel; Label and Nonnie Shapiro, my mother's teachers at the shule; my great-uncle Jake, the horseplayer and electrician.

Behind them in the photograph is a banner that reads "Branch 303 Workmen's Circle"—the Jewish Socialist fraternal order founded in the closing years of the last century. Today the organization is basically a burial society; almost all of my mother's family are in the Workmen's Circle section of the cemetery. Jack Rosenbaum from the hardware store presides—which is to say that you call him when someone dies and he knows all the plot numbers and how much money is past due on last year's upkeep and how to collect the insurance benefits and things like that. It can be a complicated business, because Uncle Itzel's side of the family is in the Branch 92 side of the cemetery—the right-wing side. Before the Russian Revolution there was only one Workmen's Circle, with more than fifty thousand members. By 1921 the split in Socialist ranks was irreconcilable. The left—the Bolsheviks, my grandfather and Uncle Jake included—started Branch 303, leaving Branch 92 to Uncle Itzel and a handful of others from the Jewish Socialist Farband who allied themselves with the English-speaking Socialist Party. Uncle Itzel has an old trunk whose contents include his speech in Yiddish introducing Eugene Debs to an audience downtown in Franklin Park, and his ribbons and delegate's badges to the Socialist Party's conventions. "After the split your grandfather and I never talked politics," Itzel says matter-of-factly—and then pauses to consider how to explain it to me. "He believed in the dictatorship of the proletariat and I didn't."

In the Washington of the 1920s, *Yiddishkeit*—the vibrant blend of Jewish secular culture that often embraced radical politics—revolved around Branch 303. The great accomplishment of my grandparents and their comrades was a camp they built in Drury, Maryland, on the Patuxent River—Camp Nit Gedayget, meaning "Not to worry," or "No worries," the same name as the big Socialist camp in Beacon, New York.

They also established the Washington shule, which, like many things in my mother's childhood, was above a store, at Seventh and O Streets. By the time I attended, the shule had moved to a ramshackle house at the other end of the Seventh Street–Georgia Avenue streetcar line and was formally known as the Cooperative Jewish Children's School of Greater Washington—the same way it was listed on the Attorney General's roster of subversive organizations for the year 1951, the first year I was enrolled.

The FBI, in its report to the Attorney General, noted:

> It is a cooperative because the parents are the management, and secular since it does not single out the principles of any one of the three main branches of the Jewish religion for instruction. It lists among its aims the teaching of the differences between the main branches of the Jewish religion and an historical appreciation of the Jewish role in the building of the United States and Israel.

The Bureau's description relied heavily on a copy of the shule's monthly newsletter, which stated that the CJCS students "wanted answers that would explain why they and their parents should be progressive Jews. They wanted to know everything about the Soviet Union, about China, about the controversies raging around the trade

32

unions and about politics in the USA. They had come to realize that in the public schools these subjects were evaded or distorted, and were grateful for this realization."

Mostly I remember being taught a smattering of Yiddish and reading books in English that explained how the Israelites had been *oppressed* by the Pharaohs and that, having been victims of oppression themselves, Jews would liberate oppressed peoples (always with an *s*) everywhere, particularly if they were black. There was no Hebrew, no Torah, and sparse mention of God. Casey Gurewitz, who went there with my mother (and testified before HUAC the same day as she), played the piano and led us in songs from an edition of *The People's Songbook* with Paul Robeson's picture on the cover. ("Casey still calls me Sylvia Walker and plays the same damn songs on the piano that he played when he was eight," says my mother.)

Had the Attorney General or the G-men who took down our parents' license numbers in the 1950s gotten inside the place they would have come away with some surprising impressions of the process of subversion. They would have learned that the vanguard of the revolution was to be marked by folk dancing. Folk dancing, it might reasonably have been inferred, was the single means of international struggle by which the working classes everywhere would rise up. By then, I suppose, much of the revolutionary fervor of my mother's era must have worn off. But we still observed the same "Jewish" holidays as she and Casey and their contemporaries: Passover (but not Yom Kippur), May Day, Paris Commune Day, July Fourth and the anniversary of the Russian Revolution—October Division. In our family only Uncle Itzel commemorates the first February uprising, the one before the Bolsheviks.

My mother dates many of the events of her childhood in relation to the birth and death of her sister. Ruth was born on August 1 of 1919. The next day my great-great-grandmother was killed while walking with my mother: a milk truck turned the corner as they were crossing the street. "My *Bubele* pushed me out of the way, but there was no time to save herself." She died at the same hospital—Garfield, now a public-housing project—where I was born.

Ruth died in February 1924—of scarlet fever or diphtheria, the doctors were never sure which. My mother remembers coming home from school on Friday and being told that her sister was sick and to gather her clothes and go to Rose and Itzel's to stay. She went upstairs. Ruth was in her bed, feverish.

My mother was asleep when the phone rang very early on Monday morning. She heard Rose and Itzel crying and saying, "What happened?" and she understood.

The day before my grandmother died—fifty-two years later—she went into a deep sleep (we had no idea how sick she was) and began talking to her dead daughter. There was a lyric playfulness in her voice that I'd never heard, a sweetness, a tenderness. "Oh, Mama," my mother said, and left the hospital room. I stayed.

"So happy," my grandmother said in her sleep. "So happy, Silvey and Ruthie—*meine shayne kinder.*"

After my grandmother's funeral we found a little box with a locket inside and a lock of Ruth's hair and her baby booties.

Ruth's grave is in the old Jewish Cemetery in Anacostia, directly across the street from where my National Guard unit used to be billeted. Alone, I stopped there after drill one day. A caretaker directed me to a ravine. I found the name WALKER and cleared away the overgrowth. There was a white headstone and on it the likeness of a little girl playing with a ball. When I told my mother about it she said Ruth was very beautiful and started to cry. She told me that's when she had become an atheist. "I decided that if there was a God, Ruth wouldn't have died—and I've never changed my mind since."

There are still Walkers all over the city, cousins and nieces and nephews of my grandfather, a disproportionate number of them engaged in the liquor business and, for reasons less explicable, in law enforcement. One homicide detective named Walker accorded me special familial passage through police cordons at various scenes of carnage and mayhem during my reporting apprenticeship, and there was even a Walker who, during that same period, was with the Washington field office of the FBI. My grandmother used to speak of him with awe—"one of the first Jews chosen by Hoover," she'd say.

The Walkers—the name had been changed from Walkowitz by the immigration officers at Baltimore—settled in Southwest Washington, the closest thing to a ghetto that existed in the capital. Its narrow streets were crowded with the commerce of immigrant experience: notions traders with their carts, egg men in their horse-drawn wagons, rag vendors, carpet merchants, building tradesmen who moved through the shape-ups on 4½ Street, the main thoroughfare of the quarter, seeking muscle for their crews. Southwest, backed against the Anacostia River, with its tiny wooden row houses built to accommodate the swelling population of Civil War Washington, was the place immigrants aspired to get out of. It was over-crowded, dirty, rough, run-down. My maternal grandmother used to speak disparagingly of the greenhorns who began in Southwest. "Our people [the Stirmans—or Stermans, as some of her six brothers and sisters spelled it] always lived in Northwest, not like *them*." And today there are Stirmans—and Stermans—all over the city, represented heavily in fine wines (wholesaling, importing) and drawn to the sale of real estate and the merchandising of imported autos, exotic coffees, and herbed cheeses.

"You didn't like her, did you?" my mother asked me recently. To the contrary, I answered. I loved my grandmother—deeply. I'm constantly surprised by moments when I find myself thinking about her, missing her. When I got laggard about phoning, she would call me at the paper. I'd get back to the office on deadline and there'd be a stack of messages, always with hers on top. "Call your grandmother. *NOW.*" And I did, usually, regardless of how close the deadline or how important the story. If too many days had passed without a byline in the paper, the message would say, "Your grandmother wants to know why you don't write anymore."

"She was a tough lady," I said at her funeral. There had been no time in her life for formal education, no opportunity for comfort, little escape from harsh economic realities. Her aspirations were for her children and her grandchildren, her nieces and nephews.

The Washington to which she and her husband came in their teens from Russia was not a city hospitable to immigrant culture. The experience of the *shtetl* and flight and exploitation were best forgotten as far as most Jews who settled in the capital were concerned; now they were Americans, or so they desired to be. Life in Washington called for a rejection of certain Old World values. Here the capitalist ideal beckoned—the notion that you could begin life as a peddler and rise to own a department store or a grocery chain. Moreover, Washington was a Southern city, with a tiny Jewish community (4 percent of the city's population in 1910) subject to all the fears associated with Southern anti-Semitism. In New York, Jews were a force to be reckoned with; more Jews resided there than in any other city in the world, they owned factories, voted in blocs, they helped define the essential character of the city. Baltimore too, forty miles to the north of Washington, was a major Jewish center with its port and immigration terminal and mills and clothing factories. But Washington had no garment district, no great industries to galvanize an immigrant labor force into trade unionism and political action. Here government was the only industry, an industry presided over by Southern oligarchs who wore straw hats and white plantation suits and refused even to let the inhabitants of their Federal District vote. There was no local government, only the District of Columbia Committees of the House and the Senate and three city commissioners appointed by the President. Jews did not figure in the basic identity of the city, nor did any other immigrant group: immigrant culture and language were antithetical to the business of government; you could hardly be a government clerk if you couldn't read or write English. So it was only natural that in Washington immigrants and their children would bend toward assimilation, acceptance, political orthodoxy.

After Ruth died, the fighting between my grandparents got worse. One drink was enough to set my grandfather off—he had no capacity for booze—but now he would down two, three shots and curse and throw things in frustration. My grandmother would stare out the kitchen window while she did the dishes and sigh Ruth's name. Later that same year they lost their home and their business. A marshal arrived at the door and tacked up a notice that my mother, then in the fifth grade, read aloud. The mortgage had become due and they owed $3,000. They had signed a contract without having it scrutinized by someone who read English. The real-estate man—they knew him from the neighborhood—had said nothing about a final $3,000 payment. They had never missed a monthly installment. Now house and store and contents were sold at auction.

Both my grandparents took jobs in the needle trades downtown: he as a tailor at Garfinckel's (he would have earned more as a fitter, but floor jobs went only to Gentiles); she as a cuffer in a pants factory, earning fifteen cents per bottom. My mother went to the place one day, to take my grandmother lunch. The "pants factory" was a sweatshop—row upon row of immigrant women and girls installed behind long tables where they did their work in stifling heat. That same year my mother had a sewing class in school; it was a home-economics requirement. Each time she took up needle and thread she would get a violent headache. Today she is still incapable of sewing a button.

My grandparents eventually saved enough to take a lease on a little shop in the basement of the Argonne, one of the big apartment houses on Columbia Road. Even in the child's eye of my memory, the shop was tiny, fifteen feet square perhaps, with a ceiling so low that adults were always in danger of hitting their heads on one of the steam pipes. Clothes were piled on almost every available inch of floor space—baled for dispatch to or from the cleaner's. My grandfather worked at the presser. The picture is fixed in my memory: his arm outstretched to the handle that pulled the mechanism down onto the pants, his foot on the steam pedal. Ooma (my earliest version of "Grandma") worked across from him—in my mother's day and mine—at the old Singer, her foot constantly in motion on the treadle, her hands maneuvering the bolts of cloth with incredible speed. When he lingered—to listen to his favorite "stories" on the radio or have a smoke on Columbia Road with the other shopkeepers or leaf through the stack of *Life* magazines in the corner—she would holler, "Tommy, get back on the machine."

My grandfather doted on my mother—"the same way he doted on you," she says, "all out of proportion. Nothing else mattered." Sundays he'd take her to Keith's vaudeville or, when she was younger, to the zoo. He and I would walk down the same big hill on Harvard Street, but first he would buy me a balloon at the top, a pink helium-filled balloon with a picture of a bear on it, and tie it around the index finger on my left hand and hold my right hand. Or we would go to Haines Point—"Speedway," my grandparents called it, I think because of the speedboats that raced around the little peninsula formed by the Washington Channel and the Potomac. When I was small, we'd go there in Popsie's Dodge—he and Itzel always owned Dodges—and sometimes we'd bring my tricycle and I'd ride along the walkway, past the men fishing for carp and rock and perch and, in the spring, shad and herring.

My mother went to Central High School. There were only five white high schools in Washington then—Eastern, Western, McKinley Tech, Business, and Central, which was the elite school in the city. Even today the building is magnificent, a huge red-brick Gothic affair set on a tract of two square blocks on one of the city's great hills. Its classrooms command a vast view past the Capitol and into Prince Georges County to the southeast. My mother, representing the Progressive Party, was among those who testified before the D.C. School Board in 1950 to urge that Central, with its tiled

38

swimming pool and greenhouses and terraced gardens and mahogany-paneled library with fireplace and leaded glass windows, be transferred to the Negro Division. Which it was, and its name changed to Cardozo, after the distinguished Jewish Justice of the Supreme Court.

She was not a good student there. Her basic ambition was to be a "government girl," a secretary in one of the federal agencies. She and her cousin Bea would cut classes together and go to the Clifton Terrace drugstore and drink Cokes and smoke cigarettes, or to Diane's Luncheonette on Fairmont Street, where there would always be a crowd. My mother was popular. There were dinner dates at young Mr. Mariott's Hot Shoppe on Farragut Street and movies and fraternity parties and Sunday afternoons spent in the crab-and-beer parlors along Route 1 in Maryland.

During high school she put a good bit of distance between herself and the shule kids who had been her closest friends for years. She pledged a sorority and saw a lot more of young people from the neighborhood. Weekday evenings she could be found on the porch of her friend Mildred Vigderhouse—"Viggy," who worked with Dita Beard at ITT when Howard Hunt came visiting in a red wig during Watergate. My mother and Viggy would sit in the swing and preen while the boys from George Washington University rode by and honked their horns. Social acceptance and approval had become more important—then, as later in her life.

Today she is very comfortable selling porcelain and crystal to congressmen and senators and diplomats and their wives, many of whom stop by the department store just to say hello if they are in the neighborhood at lunchtime.

There has always been that ambivalence.

Chapter 3

Even in grammar school, my father read a lot. Fiction. All the Algers, all of Tom Swift, the Rover Boys, O. Henry, Edna Ferber. He went to work in a circulating library when he turned fourteen, the Available Library at Broadway and 160th Street. He'd help out after school, stamp the books and take them home to read at night instead of doing his schoolwork.

His difficulties with his studies began in grammar school, P.S. 46. He wouldn't accept the discipline. "I wasn't so unlike you." This stated matter-of-factly in 1977 as if there were no record of our decade of struggle over failing grades, suspensions from school, expulsions. Once he even broke down, the only time I've ever seen it; I had just renounced any desire to go to college. He started remembering those cold Depression nights on an American Express loading dock, working to help his father pay for a Columbia education, and he cracked—huge heaving sobs. That's as near as he's ever come to saying "You owe me something." I wonder now whether part of his pain didn't come from the realization that he was appealing to some dimly perceived conception of filial loyalty. *My father sacrificed for me; I've done the same for you.* By then his aspirations for himself must have receded; I think he was terrified that I would squander my opportunity.

By the time he reached the tenth grade, at George Washington High School in Washington Heights, he had stopped going to classes almost altogether. He lived in the same block as the Polo Grounds, on 158th Street between Broadway and Amsterdam. "We went to a lot of ball games, we played on the streets, we went with girls," my father says. He and his friends would climb the rocks to Coogan's Bluff and watch the Giants and the Yankees—this was before Yankee Stadium was built in the Bronx. From their perch they could see most of the infield and the scoreboard. Sometimes they'd get inside on rain checks that the paying customers had thrown away. In his sixteenth year, he decided abruptly that he wanted to go to college—and a good one: "The fact of achievement was suddenly important." (I was the same age when he decided I ought to work. He got me an interview for a copyboy's job; he'd probably given up any real hope that I'd follow his example and make a go of school.) He enrolled in the Clark School for Concentration, despite its name a reputable institution, and made up the whole three years of high school in one year. Clark was a cram school; his Regents scores were good enough to get him into Columbia.

His initial interest in politics had nothing to do with issues. He wasn't interested in social problems, he insists. Politics was a kind of theater; even before Columbia he was drawn by the drama of the process. He can recall listening to the '24 Democratic convention on a radio in an electrician's store and being transfixed by the oratory. The oratory of the street-corner radicals—Socialists, Communists, anarchists, syndicalists—also attracted him, but he didn't know enough to distinguish among them. His first real political involvement was working as a runner for a Republican precinct captain, helping him get out the vote, stuffing literature into mailboxes. The man ran for judge in '27 and got slaughtered.

Columbia, my father told me long ago, changed his life. His undergraduate years, 1927–31, were a time of influences and ac-

41

quaintances that were lasting. He thrived on government and economics courses; he read Beard, Laski, Edward Coke on political theory; he met Dave Rein and Howie Meyer and Gene Cotton and Morty Stavis—contemporaries who were known on the Columbia campus as radicals. But he wasn't part of their crowd. "For me the ideology came later. It came out of the union movement. I hadn't read Marx at that time. I read him later, when I got to Washington."

Dave Rein, the great leftist lawyer, remembers seeing him in the tunnels under Columbia almost every day, on his knees, dice in hand. "I was interested in making enough money to get through school. That was the principal social problem of most of my friends then," says my father. "I was going to be a lawyer. It was one of the things you were supposed to be."

He graduated from Columbia University in the top quarter of his class and entered law school in 1931. He had no affinity for it. "I was lousy at it; I goofed off." When he was one course shy of graduating, he quit. "There was no self-gratification"—something I'd never associated with him; denial always seemed more in character. He went to work in the government department of Columbia as an assistant to Professor Joseph McGoldrick, a reformer who had served as comptroller of the city of New York. For two years he studied, ran seminars, graded papers. Weekends were spent at McGoldrick's house in the country, talking politics, theory, philosophy.

Meanwhile, his closest friends from law school went to Washington, among them my godfather, Ed Fruchtman, president of the class of '34, and Milt Freeman. I had lunch with Milt at the Metropolitan Club in the spring of 1978, the first time I'd seen him in twenty-five years. He had been counsel to the union. We walked over from Arnold and Porter, where he is the senior partner. Afterward my father and I had an argument. "If you want to find out what happened, that's not the place," he said. "He'll bend your ear about the Bailey loyalty case and what heroes Thurmond Arnold and Abe Fortas were for taking it. But they took only 'safe' cases, where people had no left-wing history. They never touched the tough ones." A few days later he mailed me an article from *The Nation* about liberals in the first days of the Cold War. It mentioned the Dorothy Bailey case, in which the Supreme Court upheld the constitutionality of Truman's loyalty program. "Thought this might be helpful to you," he scribbled. "Love, Dad." I think it must have been a hard note for him to write—for once he was coming to me on this subject instead of being combative. He also enclosed the latest word from the FBI:

> DEAR MR. BERNSTEIN:
> Reference is made to your pending Freedom of Information Act-Privacy Act requests. Documents pertaining to your request have been located; however, before release can be made, they must be reviewed to ascertain if they warrant classification under current standards. Due to the heavy volume of requests received, our personnel handling classification matters have accumulated a backlog of several months work. Please be assured . . .

Et cetera. The Bureau's previous letter said that the documents had been found but couldn't be released until he agreed to pay ten cents a page; and that the total would come to a minimum of twenty-five dollars. God knows what surprises would be in there. We are a family of secrets.

My father decided in the summer of '36 to return to law school and get his degree. He too wanted to go to Washington by then. He'd been to meetings protesting the Fascist invasion of Ethiopia by Mussolini's forces, he'd watched the unemployment riots, cops, marched in Union Square. And he admired Franklin Roosevelt.

"All of us, no matter how much to the left or right, considered this a special time. Washington was a very exciting place, altogether different from the kind of excitement the Kennedy people brought in, for example. It was something that had never happened in the country—at least in our times. The federal government was dealing with social problems. And you didn't have to be a clubhouse politician to get a job. I wanted to be part of it, wanted to change the world a bit." He wasn't a radical. "Reform would be the best way to describe it. Washington made me a radical."

This stated on the veranda in Bridgehampton, seated across from each other on rattan deck chairs in the summer of 1978. My father sips a vodka martini. "I wasn't very different from a lot of other guys who came to Washington then."

I'm interested in what happened to you—not the other guys. We have been around this track before.

His closest friends, the people he loves, they seem to have reasoned it out in terms of their own lives. Not he. Pushed, my father will say, "There was a Depression, the threat of fascism," as if in that sentence he has explained his life to you. Sometimes he will add, "So you did certain things."

"What things?"

"You joined the union, you organized, you joined certain fronts —maybe the Party eventually."

There is little structure to his version of events, only a hopscotch history of his times: Roosevelt, Spain, the War, the Popular Front, the CIO, Truman, McCarthy, HUAC, J. Edgar Hoover, the Marshall Plan, the Union, the Twentieth Party Congress.

To fill in the spaces, I stomp around the country, talking to his friends and contemporaries, laboring over documents in the New York Public Library and the Library of Congress, at the National Archives, the *New York Times* library, the AFL-CIO archives, the Truman Library. Trips to the Coast, retracing my parents' steps, knocking on the doors of old haunts and hangouts.

"I don't think he's given these things much thought," says his friend Abe Flaxer—head of the union when it went under; I had gone to Abe on one of those trips. "Al had a goddamn good job with the government, he had a career. Why'd he give it up to become a union official? Money didn't matter, his personal success in conventional terms didn't matter. But something happened to him in his

44

experience that led him to the belief that the best way he could pursue his life was to advance the interests of working people."

He came to Washington in the spring of '37, one of the bright young men hired by Harry Truman's friend Max Lowenthal to conduct the Senate Commerce Committee's investigation of the rail industry. He was an investigator earning two thousand dollars a year. Tex Goldschmidt, later one of Lyndon Johnson's political operatives, took him to his first union meeting, in a hall on Seventeenth Street next to Casey's Bar. The union was the United Federal Workers of America, established by a small band of dissidents from the American Federation of Government Employees in the AFL. John L. Lewis was putting together the CIO at the time; he appointed his brother Denny to head a nationwide organizing drive for government workers.

"I got interested," says my father as if that explains everything.

"Don't write now. Listen." The voice is weary and wary. "I was interested in the organization of government workers into a force. I saw the need for it. In a way it was part of the New Deal. The CIO was organizing the electorate—it was a big part of FDR's constituency. I was excited by the whole CIO movement."

He became a shop steward and started signing up low-paid white-collar workers and unskilled people; eventually he organized guards in the federal prisons, orderlies in the veterans' hospitals, welders in the navy yards, custodians and maintenance workers in the Capitol, cafeteria workers in the agencies. Many were black. He did the union work in the evenings, during lunch hours, on his leave time, calling meetings during shift breaks, talking with workers at the water cooler and waiting for the cleaning women and the elevator operators to leave at midnight.

He was excited as well by his job as an investigator. He and a hundred other young Roosevelt partisans worked out of a big bull-pen on the ground floor of the Interstate Commerce Commission Building at Twelfth and Constitution; Telford Taylor, later the chief prosecutor at Nuremberg, was assistant counsel in charge of

45

the staff; they were making headlines: Morgan and Company, Kuhn, Loeb, and half a dozen other major brokerage houses had colluded with the railroads. Fake holding companies and deceptive trusts and straw directorates had been set up to disguise the non-competitive structure of the industry, to hide the price-fixing and the rate-gouging and the joint purchases of rolling stock. Under the pressure of the investigation, the railroads began to divest. For my father the experience was a model of how the New Deal would bring about fundamental economic and political change.

Where did he see himself in this picture, what were his objectives in terms of career, what did he want to be in ten years?

"I wasn't looking ten years ahead. I was a government servant, but different from a patronage servant. I liked the kind of muckraking job I had. Did I want to be recognized and go up the ladder? Sure. But what all of us were interested in was the transformation of the political process—drafting regulations, making regulatory agencies work, establishing Social Security, the SEC, WPA, the Federal Power Commission. There was a lot of idealism at the time. We didn't think in terms of traditional political advancement. I doubt that any of us thought in career terms, of becoming Assistant Secretary. We were interested in the transformation of society. And the job and the union were both part of that process."

Book Two

Chapter 4

"The first time I went out with your father he started smoking a cigar. We were walking down Sixteenth Street to the Hotel 2400 Dine and Dance Club—and I said I didn't like cigars, I couldn't stand them. And he threw away the cigar. He didn't smoke another cigar until we were on our honeymoon, six or seven months later. We were married by Rabbi Metz in Washington. It never would have occurred to me or anyone else to do it any other way. Afterwards your father bought *The New Republic* and *The Nation* and went through all the ads in the back for a place to go on our honeymoon. We decided on Echo Lake in the Adirondacks."

This, in January 1979, in Florida. The ease and detail with which my mother discusses her life sometimes astound me. She and my father come to Miami Beach every January and February: the Conference of Christians and Jews has an annual fund-raising dinner there that my father helps organize. That winter the honoree was Walter Cronkite; the previous year, Clarence Kelley, the director of the FBI, was selected as the banquet speaker by the national office, and my father considered not working the dinner because of the choice. My sisters and I talked him out of it: he enjoys the work (and Florida) too much to sit out the winter. Fund-raising is like union organizing, he likes to say—almost convincingly.

My flight to Miami arrived late, and I reached their hotel on Collins Avenue after two in the morning. ("Mom greets me from hall in apartment, looks good, tan," it says at the top of my notes from the visit. "Dad in pajamas that don't match. Tattersall top and pinstripe bottom.") After a drink, I mentioned some material I'd located, under seal in the Federal Records Center in Suitland, Maryland—a 1951 file prepared on the union and my father by the Senate Internal Security Subcommittee. To get it I was waiting for Ted Kennedy to replace Jim Eastland as chairman of the Judiciary Committee when the new Congress convened. Records of the sub-committee can be reviewed only with signed permission from the chairman of the parent committee. I found out about the file from Jay Sourwine, who had been counsel to the Internal Security Sub-committee for years and years.

"You talked to Sourwine?" My father was incredulous. He is a very sophisticated reader of newspapers, but he has never under-stood the nuances of reporting. "Where is he?"

Reno, I answered.

"Watch it—I've got to work in that community."

I tried to reassure him.

"Sourwine is a vicious bastard," my mother interjected—in this, as in all matters, unfailingly supportive of my father. Not that her instincts were entirely wrong about Sourwine. I went to junior high school with Sourwine's son, Wayne. Nice kid. Once he invited me to dinner. I declined. I doubt that I ever mentioned it to my parents.

After Dad had gone to work that morning, my mother and I took the elevator down to the pool and found two chaises in a quiet corner. She was wearing designer sunglasses, a lavender jogging suit, and tennis shoes. My mother has never jogged to the corner, as she would be the first to tell you. "Where do you want to start?" she asked.

By lunchtime, when we broke to go to Wolfies for delicatessen, I

50

had filled a whole legal pad with notes. Years passed before I read them over again. I had given the project up in 1980—blocked, I told myself, though in almost twenty years of writing for newspapers it had never happened. Curiously, I abandoned the project in the middle of writing about her. But my mind was still on my father, or so my notes from the time indicate: "I wonder if this book isn't the equivalent of his politics, if the whole subject isn't some terrible poison, some family toxin that eats away your peace of mind—and sends your life off the tracks."

All those evenings with my father, pulling, pummeling, might have been made easier—our frustrations blunted a bit, I realize— had I gone to her first. But that is hindsight, colored by my changed perception of my mother over the intervening years. I am startled by the obviousness of some of the lessons buried with those notes for years in a packing box in the basement—and in the box of my own confusions. I've always looked too much to my father for answers when many have been nearer at hand, more accessible through her. I have always been too reluctant to see myself as *her* son as well. Yet her eye and her voice have always informed the way I see things and write. On her seventieth birthday, in 1985, I sent her flowers, giant Rubrum lilies, and a card on which I tried to say something about that. Later we talked on the phone and I told her I was reading over the interview. "There's a lot that I told you," she said.

She graduated from Central in 1933, during the economic uncertainty of the Depression. A friend in the credit department at Hecht's, the big downtown department store, told her about a job that would be available as soon as the National Recovery Act went into effect. She spent weeks waiting, letting them know she was there. Finally she was hired, at eleven dollars a week. The streetcar was eight cents then, she remembers.

At night she went to George Washington University, to get some education, nothing more; becoming a professional was not under

51

consideration. "I wanted to be a secretary—and get married, I guess." Toward that end she was still going to tea dances at the Mayflower ballroom with her cousin Bea. She went to work for the government in 1934 at the Census Bureau—doing statistics. That year there were unemployment marches in Washington; her parents put some of the marchers up, sometimes more than a dozen, in the family's rooms. She joined the Young Democrats—of the voteless District of Columbia—and went to the 1936 Democratic Convention in Philadelphia with the Texas delegation, carrying a John Nance Garner banner and riding a donkey around Sansome Street. The issues she was interested in were New Deal issues. She speaks of that time in words that parallel my father's: "The country was in very tough shape; and now this charismatic wonderful guy was President."

Not long afterward, her mother came home from a rally for the Loyalist cause in Spain and told her that the hall had been packed with young people. Her parents took her to a meeting, at the Wardman Park Hotel: Heywood Broun, the columnist and founder of the Newspaper Guild, spoke. "It was definitely my mother and father who got me interested in larger issues," she recalls with satisfaction. The crowd was so big that she and my grandparents had to sit on the steps outside the auditorium. She couldn't believe it. "This was 1937, not like when I was a little girl, when I'd been to political meetings that were almost totally Jewish, maybe thirty or forty people, most of them much older—the broken-down Old Left. This was where intellectual young people—the brightest, the most able —were. Not in the Young Democrats."

Characteristically, her commitment to this new cause became intense. She went to planning meetings, raised money, was put on the Spanish War Relief executive committee, which coordinated American support for the Loyalists. She says she had no sense of the committee being a Party front. I find this entirely believable. "I never did read Marx and Engels, nor to this day have I ever read them. But I have always had a sense of where I was on an issue. Just instinctively. I knew nothing about the CP at this point—

except, of course, that there had always been a local Communist Party and that friends of the family were in it." My mother's memory of the night Barcelona fell to Franco's troops is vivid. "There was a meeting that night," she begins. "We just sat and cried. At the Odd Fellows Hall. You knew it was going to happen, but it didn't make it any better. . . . "

In 1937 my mother applied for a job at the FBI. I know this not from her but because her application for appointment to the Bureau is in her FBI file—part of the *2,500 pages*, it turns out, that the Bureau amassed on my parents over a thirty-five-year period. They arrived through the regular mail, finally, boxes stacked knee high.

This particular document consists of eleven pages, beginning with a boilerplate statement addressed to the Director: "I hereby make application for appointment to the position indicated by the check mark, in the Federal Bureau of Investigation, U.S. Department of Justice." My mother checked the boxes for stenographer and typist, forgoing special agent and special agent/accountant. She listed her Name in Full as "Walker Irene Sylvia" and, next to a two-by-three-inch photo of herself in a large hat, signed her name "Sylvia Walker."

On June 18, the Director sent her a letter, addressed to Miss Sylvia Walker at 1644 Columbia Road, which was across the street from the tailor shop. He asked her to show up at the Justice Department on Pennsylvania Avenue for an examination and a personnel interview. The letter was signed "Very truly yours, John Edgar Hoover, Director," and the signature "J. E. Hoover" is written in quite a nice hand. It was to be the beginning of a long and difficult —and pretty much one-way—correspondence.

The next page begins, "About forty species of the fresh water clam in this country are used in the manufacture of buttons and novelties." This, I deduced, is the typing test my mother took when she showed up as requested on June 22.

She didn't get the job. Two days later, a personnel officer sent a memorandum to Clyde Tolson, the deputy FBI director, friend and confidant of J. Edgar Hoover.

RE IRENE SYLVIA WALKER—
The above applicant appeared at this office on June 22, 1937, and was afforded the stenographic and typing tests in which she received the above grade: 87 percent.

The applicant had previously appeared at this office and discussed the qualifications for the examination. She was sent here by special agent Louis Loebl of the Washington Field Division. Mr. Loebl recommended the applicant, stating she appeared to be intelligent, resourceful, and ambitious.

The applicant has only a fairly good personal appearance, is well poised, and has good personality. She does appear to be intelligent, ambitious, and resourceful, but she appears to be a bit too self-possessed. It is doubtful whether she would be amenable to discipline.

Recommendation Unfavorable.

Chapter 5

"I met your father and Uncle Eddie, your godfather, the same night. I was at a party on Fifteenth Street—a 'social' party as opposed to a 'political' one—and somebody said, 'There's a dance at union headquarters.' We went down there and these two guys were standing at the door checking out the women as they went in. Your dad was heavy, chunky, not well dressed—sloppy. His hair was black with gray, worn the same way as now. I think he's much better-looking now than then. He's aged very nicely."

This stated by the pool in Miami. Both Eddie and my father had pretty fair reputations as ladies' men, I learned later in my travels.

She started going out with Eddie right away—this was the summer of 1938. She'd see Dad at the Union Hall at the big fund-raising parties for Spanish Relief; he'd run the crap tables. "No one could possibly win," she remembers, "because the more you'd win the more he'd take off for the house—for the committee." The men she'd dated until then were all from Washington, all quite bright, but—as she puts it—they weren't interested in much of anything except living well. Ed Fruchtman and Al Bernstein had struck her immediately as different. They were from New York, they were more intellectually inclined, they went to concerts, they read widely . . . Yet there was also something familiar. "They were probably closer to the milieu that I grew up in," my mother recognizes now, and, searching for the right phrase, she says, "They were people who were interested in more than themselves."

She remembers Eddie as very handsome, very bright, and great fun, which coincides with my recollection. More than that I remember how much he and my father loved each other, their wonderful sense of adventure and affection, a certain bond that only a very few fortunate men get to share. There was no rancor when my father finally asked her out. He spotted her at a Saturday matinee at the National Theater, in the second balcony. They made a date for Monday evening—the 2400 Hotel, dining, dancing. "I had a wonderful time," my mother says. "He was *funny,* more than just fun to be with." They were engaged on April Fool's Day. She still had other dates afterward, because she didn't want to tell my grandmother. "Your grandmother didn't particularly like him; he didn't fit the formula, or mine either exactly." Appearance was terribly important to my grandmother, always. There was something about the way he carried himself—or didn't. He was short, five foot six, and he was heavy then—170 pounds, according to the FBI. My mother says she was ambivalent when he proposed—very. "I said yes because I was relaxed, comfortable with him, I had fun, there was no tension. It was the first time I felt totally accepted by anybody, and that's continued. He adored me and it was a very comfortable feeling. It still is."

That evening in Miami, after she had changed from her lavender jogging suit, we all went down to a Danish restaurant on the causeway. "My father couldn't really handle more than one drink," she had said in the afternoon, and might have said the same thing of me in the last few years. Some loose gene brings out the worst tenden-

56

cies of us Walker-Bernsteins. Not sloppy drunk, but careless, trying too hard to impress, talking too much and listening not enough, explaining, declaiming, remarking, arguing, overstating. On this occasion she was perturbed by the China policy of Frank Magrath, who runs the Miami office of the Conference of Christians and Jews —"good liberals," was how she referred in all sincerity to Magrath and his wife; they had surprised her by saying that in the infant era of Ping-Pong diplomacy with the People's Republic, the United States still had some moral obligation to the people of Taiwan. I said I agreed—as much for reasons of provocation as anything else. The pattern is well established.

Now my mother drew this latest issue in the larger terms of her perception: How could the Magraths, "so good on racial questions, so good on the McCarthy issue," be so anti-Communist?

"They have this bugaboo about Communism," she said.

"So do I," I said. What thinking person wouldn't?

The fuel for incidents such as these, I know, is stored in some vast reservoir of anger, but I have never been able to predict when it will be tapped or identify exactly the forces that release its torrents. But they were definitely present this night. Now, under the Miami moon, I told my mother that she was naive. I lectured. This is an anti-Communist country. And should be. I discoursed. About the failings of the Soviet Union, how the Soviets had killed the Socialist dream . . . In this country, I said, there is real freedom. And so on.

I have a dim recollection of my father, irritated but unfailingly reasonable, trying to recast the discussion in terms of the destruction to the country, to individuals, to democratic institutions, of the American anti-Communist obsession. The evening gets hazy after that, or so I have chosen to recall it, though I remember we somehow got off these shoals eventually and onto the safe ground of herring and codfish and causeway-smorgasbord and the desirability of eating in Jewish and Cuban restaurants in Miami.

"The same sense of fun you have with newspaper people, we had on the left," my mother said the next morning by the pool. There was no discussion of the previous night's unpleasantness. "It all flows together in my mind," she said, "the people, the causes, the activities, the organizations. We were all friendly, we had all the same interests. Your dad's centered around the union. But which was a union party and which was a Spanish party I can't remember." Joining the Communist Party wasn't part of the agenda. At least not yet. "In Washington we didn't even discuss the possibility. I felt I was doing what I wanted to do already, working for things I believed in. Your father was organizing workers. Party people had a need for intellectualizing everything, subjecting every question to a test of ideological purity. They got real physical pleasure out of it. I found it a bore, this whole business of following every twist and turn of the party line. 'Trolley-car guys,' your father used to call the ones who always had to be right on track. Everything had to be *correct*." And here she nearly spat out the word. "That was what killed the union eventually," she said. "Being correct." The union's expulsion from the CIO in 1950 was largely the result of supporting the postwar foreign policies of the USSR; commitment to the union's membership or to the precepts of trade unionism had never been at issue.

Some of their old friends continue to debate the Party line in the 1980s, regarding it with somewhat the same oracular reverence that my father accords the morning line in *The Racing Form*. I hadn't thought my mother noticed this, but I was wrong. "Miriam Rifkin is mad as a hatter on this stuff, even today. You can't be around her," she said. "She can't sleep, she's terribly upset because of what's going on in the Chinese revolution."

It is the virulence of some of their friends' criticism of America, that unchanging element of the Party line—the venom with which I have heard them sometimes assert the Soviet view of America— that, since I was a child, has always alienated me, infuriated me and, I realize now, frightened me. I have always held tightly to the belief that what distinguishes my parents from some of their friends is the absence of this poisonous point of view. But there has never been enough safety or comfort in the refuge of that thought.

"We all bought a great deal too much about the Soviet Union," my mother said sadly on that Florida winter afternoon. "We all thought it would become an *ideal* place"—though "wonderful" is the word the FBI said she used when Military Intelligence interviewed her in 1942, at J. Edgar Hoover's request. ("Subject denied that she was a Communist or was a member of the Communist Party, but she admitted that the Russian form of government was wonderful.")

My mother was working next to the White House at the time, in the War Department as a secretary in the Quartermaster Corps. J. Edgar Hoover informed the Assistant Chief of Staff for Intelligence by letter that the FBI had received "information from a highly confidential source indicating that the name of Sylvia W. Bernstein . . . appears on the active indices of the American Peace Mobilization and the Washington Committee for Democratic Action." Hoover suggested that this information warranted further investigation.

The G-2 agent who interviewed my mother concluded that she was evasive in answering questions. Nonetheless, "Agent is not prepared to state that she is a Communist." His investigation of four months turned up the fact that she "did voluntary typing and committee work about four years ago for an organization, name unknown, which was interested in helping the Spanish Loyalist cause." And he noted that "subject's husband was also a member of the Washington Committee for Democratic Action."

There was no explanation or elaboration about the breezy little remark my mother purportedly made regarding the wonders of the Soviet government. "She is interested in front organizations," the G-2 agent told his superiors, but "as long as the Communist Party line coincides with the policies and interest of this country, she may be trustworthy." He recommended that she be kept in her job and that her case be reopened for investigation only "if in the interim the policy of Russia has changed in alignment from that of this country."

J. Edgar Hoover initialed his receipt of this information, and it went into the files.

As far as I can determine (the Bureau's record-keeping being a little less than orderly at times), this correspondence represents the first red flag waved by the FBI about either of my parents. From subsequent entries it appears to have set in motion the extensive surveillance, investigation and reporting back to FBI headquarters about my parents that occurred at least every six months over the next thirty years.

As the files of the FBI note, my parents moved to San Francisco in July 1942, when my father was appointed senior West Coast investigator for the Office of Price Administration. It is not true, as some accounts would have it, that one of the people he supervised was Richard M. Nixon. Nixon worked elsewhere for OPA. My father, when he took the job, was also designated by the union as its principal organizer on the Coast.

"In San Francisco the peer pressure to join the Party was incredible," my mother said by the pool, without a hint of the defensiveness her words might suggest. She thinks she remembers my father saying, "This might be a problem," on their way out west. Still, they were both clear in their minds "that this was something we were not going to do."

I picked this moment to ask my mother whether she had wanted a revolution in this country—a question that is probably more revealing of a 1950s education in Washington than it is of anything else.

"I always thought by peaceful means . . . public ownership of the means of production . . . Look, I'm in a different stage of my life now. I'm comfortable. I'm not sure my feelings are the same."

She sighed. "What happened to us would have happened anyway, without the CP membership. We wouldn't have talked before Congress. You gave up an awful lot for being *accused* of this—maybe that's why your dad won't discuss it." Now her voice became different. Suddenly the jogging suit and the designer sunglasses disguised nothing. "If you center on this I think it's going to shatter my life again," she said, and I could see that her face was trembling.

The tone hardened. "People your age are writing their autobiographies. What do you think you have to contribute by writing about this? What makes you think it's interesting? You and your sisters go to shrinks and things, you analyze and you inspect. Your father and I prefer to *do* things in our lives. We're not introspective. We're more interested in people."

And, for the first time in my life, I heard my mother really imploring. "You have to believe me that your father's loyalty—his interest, his passion, his commitment—was to the union. From when I first knew him."

She talked about my father organizing the guards at Alcatraz and what a great moment that was. Then she talked about "how much I really adore him" and started to cry. "This union was the cause he worked in. His sole interest was the union and workers. He looked at it from the perspective of labor and management. He didn't need any directives from the Party fellows, the way some of the union's leaders did. The thing about the Party was that it was never important—it was just there," she said. "There was nothing *subversive* about it. That is what I resent most—the idea that there was something sinister. They did a lot of good things," she says of the Party and the fronts and committees and causes she and my father supported.

Chapter 6

I arrived in San Francisco twelve weeks after the visit to Florida. San Francisco, my mother had said, had been a different kind of city—militant, active, open. "You didn't have the terribly scared, clandestine thing you had in Washington." The San Francisco to which they came in July 1942 was a union town, dominated by organized labor—and the left—as no other American city was then or has been since. Retracing their steps, hearing the words and voices of their friends, climbing the great hills of the city, I was able to catch something of the excitement. For the first time, I was able to feel a real connection with their life then.

> On November 9, 1942, San Francisco T-2 advised that there seemed to be a concerted movement among the employees of the Office of Emergency Management and the Office of Price Administration in San Francisco to organize and affiliate with the CIO. T-1 stated that in this endeavor, ALFRED BERNSTEIN, SYDNEY FEINBERG, GENEVIEVE BLUE AND DORIS MARASSE appeared to be the ringleaders, and in the opinion of T-1 they were closely affiliated with the Communist Party. T-1 at this

time named the leader, BERNSTEIN, as openly claiming that everything is wrong with all Government and that they will continue to be wrong until employees, through unionization, take over and operate these agencies of the government. The group had affiliated with the CIO and demanded that its Bargaining Committee be recognized.

A pretext telephone call to the former address of the subject disclosed that . . . in 1942, BERNSTEIN came from 3806 Davis Place, N.W., Washington, D.C., to San Francisco, where he entered on duty as a supervisor of investigation in the Office of Price Administration.

San Francisco T-3 advised in February, 1942, that BERNSTEIN was the instigator of many informal union meetings held in the OPA office during office hours.

On February 21, 1943, Special Agent observed an automobile registered to ALFRED BERNSTEIN, 762 DeHaro St., San Francisco, parked in the vicinity of the home of Louise Bransten, where THE TOM MOONEY LABOR SCHOOL was having a cocktail party.

The Daily People's World, a Communist dominated West Coast newspaper, issue of April 22, 1943, carried an advertisement which stated that the Seamen were having a spring party at 762 DeHaro Street on April 25. This address was listed to ALFRED BERNSTEIN.

An acquaintance of SYLVIA WALKER BERNSTEIN revealed that while residing at San Francisco in 1942 with her husband, she was employed by Locals 2 and 10 of the International Longshoremen's Union and also by the alleged Communist law firm of Gladstein, Grossman, Margolis, Sawyer and Edises. . . . During 1943 Mrs. Bernstein was employed by the reported Communist front organization, the Committee on Free Elections.

The Daily People's World, issue of June 1, 1943, carried an announcement by ALFRED BERNSTEIN, national executive board member of the United Federal Workers of America, to the effect that an organizing drive of UFWA in Northern California would be launched. . . .

I spent several afternoons with Helen Fruchtman, my godfather's widow, who had come to San Francisco in 1943 to help run the CIO canteen and had frequently visited my parents in their house on Potrero Hill. "At the time we were all younger than you are now," she said. Somehow it had never occurred to me. . . .

Some evenings I'd take the BART train over to Berkeley and sit in Jessica Mitford's kitchen while she rummaged through boxes of old pictures and union bulletins and mimeographed song sheets: faded battles and causes and parades memorialized in verse and exhortation and sepia tincture. In her memoir *A Fine Old Conflict* she had written about my father: "Al Bernstein signed me up as a member of the United Federal Workers union. He and I had adjoining desks [at OPA], and shared a propensity for sloppiness that was the despair of the administration."

Decca took me to dinner at the home of Doris Marasse Walker— Dobby. She had been president of the union under my father's tutelage. Other old friends were there: Merle and Al Richmond; in the forties and fifties he had been editor of *The People's World*. From Dobby's living room I could look out over the docks where my father shipped out for the South Pacific. "He was a most unlikely soldier," said Dobby. "Al was an investigator at OPA and I was a sorority girl just out of law school at Berkeley when we met. He arrived after we began to organize. He had a lot of experience— skills and insights about how political people functioned in a union. He gave me my first and best lessons in trade unionism. He became my mentor. He taught me trade-union principles."

Decca described him as "the force in the union, the one whose opinion was listened to the most," and, with astonishment, she told the tale of him organizing the Alcatraz guards—a tale, I was to learn, that had become a piece of folklore in the San Francisco labor movement.

64

I listened, unsure of what I had come to find, hardly asking questions.

"He was a great investigator," Dobby said. "He enjoyed that. But he was much more interested in the union. My first introduction to Potrero Hill was visiting them. They gave great parties. I remember him with his big cigar and a smile on his face and ashes all over his jacket." She got up and, from the window, pointed to their house on De Haro Street.

I cannot remember exactly what my thoughts were: the war, the warmth in that room, troopships, my mother, young, not yet thirty. I wrote in my notebook, aware that I was looking at the house where I was conceived.

When I sat back down at the dining table the others were still talking about the parties. And the poker. Hot and heavy poker, almost every night. Ann Dimond, an OPA lawyer whose ex-husband had been one of my father's closest friends at Columbia, remembered asking Richard Nixon into the game. But he declined, she said. "He was too stiff."

"Everybody remembers that period with pleasure," said Merle Richmond. With my mother, she had been a secretary at Gladstein, Grossman, Margolis et al. "We worked together, shared a point of view and a lot of warmth. Your eyes are like hers," she said. "She was trustworthy, but, the most important thing, she was fun. She's a very bright woman—with sparkle. She was quite different from most of the people I worked with in the office. Some of them were pretty grim—the CP people tended to be pretty grim. And she was not. She didn't throw her weight around and she knew how many beans made five. Politically she held the line. I think Sylvia was very much like me: a gut identification with the cause, but without theory. I can see her, her black hair sort of wavy, her smile. Her wit—a sense of play and energy. She was a mensch."

The matter-of-fact way in which everyone discussed the Party, and its relationship to the union, surprised me.

Both Dobby and Decca said they had assumed, by the positions he took on various issues, that my father was already a Party member when he arrived in San Francisco. But neither had known for certain.

"The enemies [of the left] always said that the union was a front, and in a sense it was," said Decca. "In California, the whole CIO under the leadership of Harry Bridges was Communist-dominated. But the federal workers were not high on the Party's list of priorities." Bridges, president of the International Longshoremen and Warehousemen's Union, was the commanding figure of the West Coast labor movement. The government spent years trying to have him deported, on grounds he was a member of the Communist Party.

Patiently Dobby explained to me, "You must remember that we're not looking at the union as an end in itself. The union, to a Communist, in addition to bettering the workers' condition, is also a means of making them class-conscious. So if you are in a union it's hard to draw the line sometimes between simple economism and narrow left sectarianism. Our dilemma was, How do you carry out the primary purpose of a union and also create class struggle?"

Picturing my father in this context was somewhat difficult.

A few days later, my father phoned me. The Christians and Jews, it seemed, were having trouble with their San Francisco fund-raising campaign; he'd be arriving the next morning.

> May 29. Well, Dad has a different view, though to what degree I'm still not sure. Certainly as far as his own participation was concerned. Yes, he was in the Party but he didn't take orders from anybody when it came to the union. This was a trade union, committed to trade-union principles. The question of members' affiliation, of whether the leadership was in the Party, was incidental, etc. Sounds like hair-splitting to me. Yet some of the distinctions he makes are important. But there is some other point he is trying to make about the union and himself, something I can't put my finger on, some important shading or gradation that made

66

things more complicated than other people have indicated. But that will have to wait.

My notes on the next day begin with a description of the city at twilight from the Top of the Mark: bejeweled, twinkling, a dazzling confluence of water and sky and peak. My father and I were waiting for Dobby to join us for dinner. Over a drink, I told him that people were discussing the Party, and what they did in it, with no prodding from me.

Who?

Dobby, Decca, the Richmonds, Helen Fruchtman . . . I listed others. Everybody, I said.

"That's out here. Washington is different. Your mother and I are more part of the Establishment than the people you've seen here."

I told him—more strenuously than before—that I saw no way to avoid dealing with questions about the Party.

"A lot of people went to jail rather than talk about it," he said. "It's a principle." At which point Dobby arrived. There was some brief talk about old friends (my favorite "aunt" had lost all her money playing poker in Gardena), about Mom, about the city. Dad said he had taken the cable car for a nickel, the senior-citizen fare. Dobby—ten years younger than he, short, handsome in a rugged way, boyish—was amused. I was struck by how much they liked being together. Earlier Dobby had said to me, "You knew you were going to have a good time around your dad and it was going to be interesting." Until Dobby arrived I had been anticipating another rancorous go-round with my father. Now to him she pronounced her enthusiasm for my inquiry and filled him in on some of the ground we had covered.

I thought I saw an opportunity to convince him. Finally people from the Old Left were being accorded real respect and honor, I began. (This was in the spring of 1979, before the era of Ronald Reagan.)

Dobby's face soured. My father called me naive: It was true only of those presumed to have been non-Communists, he said.

Dobby nodded. "Today anybody accusing the American Communists or the Soviet Union has the full tilt," she maintained. "The Cold War, the McCarthy period and the decline of the CP make it damn near impossible to get over the barriers of prejudice. Today anybody who attacks the CP or the Soviet Union will be heard. Things are being said about the USSR that are more extreme than anything in many years."

I cited the success of Decca's book as evidence of a new attitude: a willingness to pay attention to what these people had to say.

But in the last analysis, my father pointed out, Decca's book is really about why she *left* the Party. In fact, the book trivializes the whole experience of having been in the Party, reducing it to almost farcical anecdote.

"People today are saying you were courageous but a horse's ass if you were in the Party," my father said.

"Or at least that we were quixotic," Dobby added.

I remembered and repeated my father's remark about Lillian Hellman not opening herself up to that kind of embarrassment.

To which Dobby appended, "I don't think you can really deal with our generation without dealing with why we supported the Soviet Union and why U.S. policy was so anti-Soviet. But it won't be a very popular book if you do it. You can't fail to come out with an analysis that is highly critical of U.S. foreign policy. There is no way to write without dealing with current problems." And she asked me, "Where are you on China? On Ethiopia? On the Sudan? On Afghanistan? On Bangladesh?"

"Jesus Christ," I wrote in my notebook.

"I've always been an issue-oriented guy," my father said later, over espresso in North Beach. Dobby had gone home. Now he seemed to want to talk—cautiously, but I recognized the desire to get me to understand. We had been for a walk. And in his step there seemed a spiritedness, in his voice a resonance.

"Affiliation never meant anything to me when I was in the Party," he was saying now. "I never had anything to do with the apparatus. I'm a lot like Izzy . . ." And he talked about his old friend I. F. Stone, the great journalist—who had never been a Party member. "Izzy once told me that in the early fifties, before he started publishing the *Weekly,* he thought about going to live in Israel permanently. But he decided it wouldn't work because he'd have to depart from an ideological line." My father drew no further parallel, just paused for the import.

There is a scene in the movie biography *I. F. Stone* in which my father speaks of Izzy's values; then the camera cuts to the next generation: to me, talking about how *I. F. Stone's Weekly* was always in the house during my childhood and how, much more than the *Washington Post* or the *Star,* I had looked to it to tell me what was going on in the world.

"There were unions and all kinds of front organizations which people were in because they believed in the issues," my father continued now. "I basically believed in the trade-union movement. I never had any problem with *not* joining the Party. Out of the trade-union movement I took some stands on international issues—fronts, the League against War and Fascism."

So why had he joined the Party in 1942 when he got to the Coast? I asked.

"I became a union leader there. I got involved with the Party. My view was simple at the time I joined. I was interested in the union. I was a labor leader, and a good part of the labor movement on the West Coast, the leadership, was leftist—members of the Party. I knew these guys. I worked with them. But I was only a half-assed member of the Party. I went to a couple of meetings."

I recalled something said to me by Bob Treuhaft, Decca's husband, who for many years had been Dobby's law partner: "There was a feeling that unless you joined and were with us you were the enemy."

"I think your focus on the Party is cockeyed," my father said. "You're up the wrong tree. The right tree is what people did. I was involved in this kind of union which had left manifestations and followed the leftist line. But our union wasn't a Communist union. You might have had a guy near the top who was a member, who was fairly high up . . ." and here he talked about a couple of occasions when one of the union's officers "was like a goddamned dope" for taking some stand or another that followed the Party line, particularly after the war. Among other things, the union had opposed the Marshall Plan.

"I worry about your premise. The *right* premise, the premise of a lot of recent books about the period, is that people were persecuted because of what they did, not because of their affiliation. Because once you admit affiliation you get into all that Stalinist crap."

It seemed to me that "all that Stalinist crap" was a pretty legitimate subject for inquiry.

"Once you get into that you lose the point," he said.

Why couldn't he trust me not to lose the point? I argued. I'd been around for a while as a journalist.

"The persecution came because people *did* things. Just remember that these people you're talking about were in the forefront of civil rights, women's rights. People on the left were really the pioneers to make Washington, D.C., an open city, and that caused a great deal of enmity. I could have been the same kind of guy without becoming a member of the Party. Read the Bailey case. She wasn't a member."

I said I'd get slammed—rightly—if I did what he was advising.

When my father feels something intensely he will sometimes put his hand to his cheek and rub it unconsciously, as if trying to push up his forehead and unfurrow his brow. This was one of those moments. "I think you do a disservice if you do this," he said. "You're muffing the problem; you're going to write about political oppression from the wrong perspective. The premise people even-

70

tually accepted after the McCarthy period was that the victims weren't Communists. If you're going to write a book that says McCarthy was right, that a lot of us were Communists, you're going to write a dangerous book. You're falling into a trap," he warned. "Because we were bad guys according to McCarthy's standards. And those were the standards then and they prevail now."

What people had actually done and the fact that some of them had joined the Communist Party were two separable issues, I maintained.

"Was I 'oppressed' because I was a Communist?" He posed the question and answered it. "No. It was incidental. I was 'oppressed' because of what I did, because I was affiliated with a left-wing union.

"You're going to prove McCarthy right, because all he was saying was that the system was loaded with Communists. And he was right. You've got to take a big hard look at what you are doing. Because the whole fight against him was that people weren't Communists."

McCarthy, of course, hadn't known who were Communists and who weren't.

When I take notes I have a habit of drawing a box and, inside it, putting my own observations about an event or an interview—to separate them from the running stenographic account. Inside such a box I now scribbled: "Big pblm: How to be honest and not hurt people."

He continued, "I'm worried about the kind of book you're going to write and about cleaning up McCarthy. The problem is that everybody said he was a liar; you're saying he was right."

Not so, I protested. I was saying people had no idea of what people who were Communists actually did. At least this little group of people, many of whom, as he put it, happened to be Communists.

"I'm telling you what's going to happen—and I'm a pretty sharp guy on some of these things," my father said. "I agree that the Party was a force in the country. But if you start with the premise that the CP was central—"

71

He was presuming that the truth is counterproductive, I said, that it's damaging. I couldn't make that assumption or work that way. Then I said something self-serving about applying to journalists Lillian Hellman's statement about not cutting one's principles to fit the day's fashion.

"Listen," he said, "her lawyer went with her to that hearing and he knew she had been a member of the Communist Party and the reasons he gave for not letting her testify were quite good ones. But they are not good enough for you."

She wasn't repentant enough, her lawyer, Joseph L. Rauh, Jr., had told her.

My father did not want me to imply anything untrue, that he had *not* been in the Party, for example, or even that he had been uncomfortable with the Party's basic policy positions on many international issues (the major exception being the Hitler-Stalin Pact, which both my parents had opposed, to the extent of joining an organization that expressed its opposition; by the time they entered the Party, Russia was at war with Germany).

"I'm saying that if you write a book in which you state that your characters are Reds, then there's some consequences to it. If you write a book in which you don't talk about formal affiliations, in which you talk about what people stood for—that's different. But you can't be the Un-American Committee and say who was and who wasn't."

And that, I suppose—looking at it now—is the crux of the problem. Today I would answer that it is possible to do both: be truthful, talk about formal affiliation (if individuals are willing to) and examine that affiliation (and people's lives) in terms of what they actually did.

That evening I was not so hopeful.

This is really pissing me off, I said.

"Why not say—it's pretty simple, Carl—" he has always known how to write this story—"that I was part of a force. And I was in the labor movement and I said everything that I wanted to say without revealing my political affiliations. Because if I had revealed my political affiliations I'd lose my effectiveness—and that still goes today."

I looked at him. And said that for the first time he was saying something not disingenuous about his motives in shutting off this line of inquiry.

"Basically people don't talk about political affiliations, because it still brings the same reaction today," he insisted. "And what I accomplished in those days is going to be demeaned, what I accomplished is going to be undone. What was my purpose, my *real* purpose? people are going to ask. Who was I really serving in that union?" No book, he said, is strong enough to offset that.

"The whole folklore of the country holds that the CP wanted to overthrow the government. I don't want to buck that at my age."

Was it ever committed to the overthrow of the government? I asked.

"I don't think so," he said. "Certainly I don't believe it. I never met anyone who believed in that. And I was in a labor organization. It all stems from argument over a lot of theoretical crap." He paused.

"I think this name-calling is a dangerous process," my father said. "Just because a guy paid his dues . . ."

If all it involved was paying dues, why not say so?

"My own dealings were I went to a dozen meetings and did nothing. I went to one important meeting. I wasn't involved in anything at the Party level. If the Party had anything to do with my union, I don't know about it. If some guy got up in my union and said, 'The CP line is such and such,' I'd say it's a lot of nonsense. It's much more loose than anything you imagine, the relationship of the Party and the union. I held a very important job in the union, but as far as a policy-making role, somebody imposing a line on me, it's a lot of crap."

And he added, "I think you're being romantic about these present times. I think you've been in San Francisco too long."

And today, recalling our conversation, it makes me feel queasy, a little bit like an Eastland or a McCarthy.

73

Finally my father said, "I don't want you to write a dishonest book. But I don't want you to write an evil book either."

And the FBI concluded:

> In 1943 an investigation was made relative to Alfred Bernstein in view of the fact that Source M, reliability not given, advised of rumors he had concerning Bernstein which Source M believed might indicate Bernstein was engaged in subversive activities. There was no indication, however, that Bernstein was involved in the above matters.

Book Three

Chapter 7

We lived on Chesapeake Street. My father was working at home.
He'd work in the dining room during the day, scribbling on yellow
legal pads. This was around 1949, 1950. And then in the evening
people would come to the house. They seemed frightened.

I was explaining this to Woodward. He had been reading the
manuscript.

"I'm trying to figure out how you're going to land all these airplanes," he said. He was writing about the CIA.

And so we edged back to familiar routine: a summer of writing
and passing typed pages back and forth and asking each other what
things meant and telling each other to dig deeper. Thirteen summers earlier we had done this in Florida, at a house his mother
owned on the Gulf Coast. This summer there were a couple of
weeks in Washington, some days caught in Sag Harbor, a few more
in Manhattan. And a long car ride, from Georgetown to the Chesapeake Bay and back—with the tape running.

"Okay, so what else was nice about Howdy Doody?" Woodward
asked at one point. He is nothing if not thorough.

"Buffalo Bob," I answered. "And Princess Summer/Fall/Winter/Spring—she'd be cavorting around with next to nothing on. . . . Yeah, it was a club. Everybody sat in the Peanut Gallery and it was a sense of belonging."

The test was loyalty, I explained. In 1947 Truman had issued Executive Order No. 9835. It decreed that a person who was perceived to be disloyal couldn't hold a government job. The term "loyalty" was not defined. A Federal Employees' Loyalty-Security Program was established. Automatically the suspect employee was notified of his or her possible dismissal from the government. And informed of the right to a hearing before his or her agency's loyalty board. The loyalty board determined finally who was loyal and who wasn't. Accused could not confront accuser; in fact, the accused never learned the identity of the accuser—only that an allegation of disloyalty had been made. There were 12,859 of these cases filed between 1947 and 1953.

More than five hundred were handled by my father in his capacity as director of negotiation for the union. He won about 80 percent of them. It was the closest he came in his life to practicing law.

I have the transcripts of a couple hundred of these star-chamber proceedings, carbons typed on onionskin (for this was before the age of Xerography) and preserved in textured blue folders. My father's handwritten notes—the interviews, his preparation and his observations—are tucked inside, the hand surprisingly like mine, seemingly illegible upon confrontation, then yielding itself upon examination, the tortured bends and turns flowing somehow into coherence and purpose. They smell of mold and rot, these records buried first in the dank of the basement on Chesapeake Street and then under the steps in Silver Spring. Yet the memory of my father making those notes is as vivid as if his pen had scratched them yesterday; and though I had scant idea then of what he was writing, I am sure that my perception of the atmosphere was accurate, even

78

barometrically precise, and that it measured perfectly the storms gathering in our lives.

The house was narrow, two stories and an unfinished basement: four little bedrooms and a single bathroom upstairs; kitchen, dining room, and living room on the ground floor. We moved there when my father came home from the war. A tattered wing chair stood in the far corner of the living room, where I'd scrunch up and suck the index finger of my right hand while rubbing my left ear with the other hand. (Now my finger has a crook in it.)

All I knew was that people came every evening to see him and that he wrote down a lot of notes and that these strangers were in some kind of trouble and arrived very upset. Often they had little kids with them, who would be put down in a bed here and a bed there. The visitors stayed until late into the night, until the grown-ups were calm and whatever business at hand had gotten taken care of. My mother would bring food in. And she'd comfort the wives and husbands.

I remember my father being reassuring. Very reassuring. "All right," he would say—and this I was told thirty years later by many of the people who passed through those rooms, for they became my parents' closest friends and the people I knew best through my childhood—"all right, we have to deal with this in terms of what the facts are. Straighten out the facts first." Warmth. And healing. That was the sense they came away with. Some nights, at the same table, there would be poker games, with chips dispensed from an oak box that had sat in the corner of my Grandfather Bernstein's dining room. Before I'd go to bed I'd clamor for my own and be handed a stack of them. They felt good to the hand—hard, and bright with color: red, white and blue, each with a heart in the middle. And so, from Bob Weinstein, the union's director of organization, I acquired my nickname: Chips.

My next memories are of getting the television set. And roller-skating all the way down Chesapeake Street. Chesapeake was this great black-topped street, and all of it went downhill because the reservoir and the river were down at the bottom of River Road, which ran roughly parallel. You could go half a mile on roller skates, coast all the way. Each summer Chesapeake would be freshly black-topped. I'd roll down to Forty-fifth Street, to Barbara Bennett's house—her father owned the grocery at the corner of Wisconsin and Brandywine—to watch television, because we didn't yet have a television set. I'd always watch Howdy Doody. Howdy Doody had freckles and I had freckles and I had won a freckle contest at Glen Echo, the local amusement park. This was in the days before the picket lines went up around Glen Echo. It was a Howdy Doody–lookalike contest, and I'd gotten to squirt Clarabelle with the seltzer bottle. And I had agitated greatly thereafter for a television set of our own.

Then one day, a Sunday, my father and I went to play miniature golf.

The miniature golf course was on Wisconsin Avenue, across from where Neiman-Marcus is now. The windmill hole was approximately on the spot where the Hamburger Hamlet bar stands today. My father was bending over to putt through the windmill when I got this pretty good notion to take a whack at his head with a golf club. It is the only time in my life I consciously remember feeling like that. My sister Laura had just been born. Probably it was Oedipal nonsense. But in my family Marx and Freud get very confused.

Sometimes when I think of that moment I get very upset, for I had in fact been possessed with a sense that I was powerful enough to dispatch him. I was wound up and ready to do it. Anyway, I was glad I hadn't done it, because when we came home a television set was in the living room. And the television set was there because of whatever it was my father had been doing for these people who were coming to see us in the nighttime. They had gotten together and given our family a twelve-inch Dumont TV.

80

Chapter 8

Some of their most basic decisions suggest a curious ambiguity toward radical commitment, even a desire to be isolated from the intensity of collectivist experience. Whether by design or circumstance, my parents always resisted the geographical cohesiveness of the Washington left. Following the war, their friends had clustered in Trenton Terrace, a wretched new development of small Colonial-style brick apartments built across the Anacostia in Southeast Washington. The House Un-American Activities Committee, in a 1954 report, described the enclave as "a leftist nest," and however offensive the language, the characterization was not far off the mark.

We lived on the other side of town in the wonderful isolation of St. Ann's Parish, in a stucco shoebox designated "semidetached" by the real-estate agents. It was in fact *attached*—by popcorn-thin walls to the Kalowar family. Mr. Kalowar was from the Philippines, had a gold tooth, and had gone to work as a civilian clerk for the Army after the war. My friend Freddie Kalowar and I both wore satin warm-up jackets that his brother-in-law Gene had brought back from a tour of duty in the Navy: bright blue with "Okinawa" stitched on the back in mock-Japanese characters above a garishly embroidered map of the island.

Life in that neighborhood, with its predictable rhythm and flow, was idyllic—seemed so then and even more so afterward. What made it that way, I think, was the sheer ordinariness of the existence, the absence of the kind of complexity and confusion and conflict that shaped life beyond. We kept a duck, Mr. Peepers, in our backyard; we never locked the doors. Mr. Robey, the milkman, had his midmorning coffee at our breakfast table. For a while Dad seemed to have time on his hands. I didn't know why, only that it made me feel good, this chance for the two of us to be together. Some afternoons I'd come home from school and find him at the dining table, jotting on a notepad, and we'd go outside and have a catch, Dad neglecting to take the cigar out of his mouth, ashes flying when he released the ball, a big smile across his face.

Though I attended the neighborhood public school, most of my friends went to St. Ann's—children whose fathers were salesmen or clerks or barbers or bus drivers. Buzzy Bastable's father, Frank, had been a Yankee second baseman and now he scouted for the Richmond farm club; Johnny Gianaris' uncle was one of Rocky Marciano's trainers (his other uncle was Pete Gianaris, who ran the town's numbers rackets); our idols were the Luce brothers, both four-letter men at Woodrow Wilson High. Each spring and summer evening, we played Indian ball in Forty-third Street until there was barely enough light to see the ball roll at the bat and jump at your face. In fall and winter there was football. Apprised of my ineligibility for the St. Ann's team, I carried my aspirations to the Phoebe Hearst Indians in Cleveland Park—presumably the only football team in the world named for the mother of William Randolph Hearst. The evening after the first practice I asked my father whether he would buy me a uniform. The cost was twenty-two or twenty-three dollars, as I remember, a little more than the week's groceries. There was no guarantee I'd make the squad, I told him. He said yes without hesitating. During the scrimmages of the next few weeks I picked myself off the ground thinking that somehow I had to prove myself

82

to him, win his approval, come through. Not that he articulated anything resembling pressure or expectation. But still I felt it. Or rather, as I recognize now, I imposed it on myself. I remember almost nothing about what happened on the field that season, but retain instead an indelible image from the father-and-son prayer breakfast at the Wisconsin Avenue Hot Shoppe preceding the opening game: my father tapping his foot uncomfortably while the whole lot of us ten-year-olds and our dads got prayed over by the rector from St. Columba's, my father's arm around my padded right shoulder, proud.

Many years later, rereading a story in the paper that I thought I had underreported, I remembered that breakfast. And realized that it is my father for whom I write, whose judgment I most respect, whose approval I still seek. And that perhaps the time had come to unburden myself of that.

Chapter 9

My most pervasive memory of those two summers is of the heat. That oppressive Washington heat. This was before air-conditioning, or at least before anyone I knew had air-conditioning at home, 1951, '52. In her history of black Washington, *The Secret City*, Constance McLaughlin Green devotes a few lines to what happened those summers, but she doesn't mention the heat.

> . . . The campaign [to desegregate] downtown restaurants began after the report of the National Committee on Segregation drew attention to the "lost" anti-discrimination laws of 1872 and 1873. . . . Members of the Citizens Committee for Enforcement assembled statistics on how many out of 99 restaurants in downtown Washington denied service to well-behaved colored or racially mixed groups, how many accepted them, and in either case what the proprietors' reasons were and how white patrons reacted. Under the guidance of Annie Stein, an energetic young white woman, and further inspired by the nonagenarian Mary Church Terrell, the surveying groups, each composed of three or four

people, were at pains never to argue with waitresses or managers and left quietly if they were rebuffed.

Actually it was only at the beginning of the campaign that we left quietly when we were rebuffed. "Negotiate, boycott, picket." That was the strategy Annie Stein had devised. I hated the whole enterprise. I was seven years old. Thursdays and Saturdays I'd be ripped from the neighborhood, torn from the day's game of stepball or running bases, and placed on a streetcar that took me and my mother to the little law office that Joe Forer and Dave Rein shared downtown across from the Trans-Lux Theatre on Fourteenth Street. There Annie Stein would tap me on the head and say, "Now, honey, this is so-and-so," and pair me with a Negro child. The black children usually wore church clothes, little girls in pink and white and lace and patent leather, boys with too-long clip-on neckties hanging from starched collars, jackets neatly buttoned. Today when I see black children dressed for the Easter Parade I am reminded of those children.

Thirty years after the fact, it is difficult to convey—much less comprehend—that slow, drawled, hazy small-town atmosphere of midcentury Washington. I went to a segregated public school; all the city's playgrounds and swimming pools were segregated; the hotels were for whites only, except for the Dunbar, way up on Fifteenth Street across the city's old Boundary Avenue; the wards of the municipal hospital were segregated; the only integrated theater in town was the Gayety Burlesque house on Ninth Street.

There had always been Negroes in and out of our house, and from the outset I had been taught that for them life was defined by struggle and filled with injustice. The Negroes I knew best were the Richardson family. Tommy Richardson was vice president of my father's union; his father, whom I knew only as Mr. Richardson, was a redcap at Union Station and a member of the Brotherhood of Sleeping Car Porters. Marie Richardson, Tommy's sister, was going to jail; my father and Joe Forer were trying to keep her out, I knew.

85

My perception was that this had something to do with her being a Negro. It wasn't until I was a little older, when I would go with my father on Sundays to call on Mr. and Mrs. Richardson in their little rowhouse on Florida Avenue, that I began to understand that Marie was in jail because of something having to do with being a Communist. In fact Marie was doing twenty-eight months to seven years for having falsely signed a non-Communist affidavit when she applied for a clerical job at the Government Printing Office. Such distinctions were too subtle for me at age eight, a bundle of loose ends I could never get tied right: Negroes, Communists, Jews, civil rights, civil liberties, Russia, spying, the Cold War . . .

Sundays, after visiting the Richardsons, I would be hauled off to the shule, where a few hours of discussion about the Israelites, W. E. B. Du Bois, and Abraham Lincoln did little to clarify things. We studied the report of the President's Committee on Segregation in the Nation's Capital, a thin blue volume with a picture on the cover of the Great Emancipator sitting in his temple at the end of Memorial Bridge. Agonizing in its detail, the report enumerated the indignities and cruelties of Negro life in Washington.

By then people in Washington were becoming aroused by the demonstrations downtown. One Sunday, after shule, my sisters and I were packed into the dilapidated family Plymouth for another union picnic that Annie Stein had organized in the field behind Trenton Terrace. Annie and Arthur Stein were my parents' closest friends—Artie was treasurer of the union. But this time it was more than just my father's union and the same familiar faces. A movement was building. A lot of white people there had read in the newspapers about what was happening downtown. People came from the Government Cafeteria Workers Union, the Sleeping Car Porters, the Hotel and Restaurant Workers, the black churches and, according to the FBI files on my mother and father, the Progressive Party; my father was chairman of its antidiscrimination committee, Annie was secretary—facts noted in the FBI reports. It is my recollection that Paul Robeson sang at the picnic, but that isn't reflected in the files. Pete Seeger's presence is noted, however. I remember he sang

86

"Which Side Are You On," and (before everybody joined hands for "Solidarity Forever") he introduced a version of Leadbelly's "Washington's a Bourgeois Town," with the words changed to "Washington's a Jim Crow Town."

The Trans-Lux had air-conditioning. Next to the ticket window a big sign announced in shimmering blue-tinsel-icicle lettering, "It's Kool Inside." Some evenings, after trying to get served in the restaurants on F Street, my mother and I would go to a movie to cool off. *Kon-Tiki* was playing that summer. I did not understand why it was okay to patronize the Trans-Lux and not Neisner's Luncheonette, but I was grateful for the relief. These were long days. Occasionally, instead of going to the movies, we would go to visit my great-grandmother. She lived above Singer's Haberdashers on Seventh Street. A tiny woman dressed in black, with wrinkled skin and pierced ears, she had been a *hebamme,* a midwife, but now all she did was walk back and forth to the synagogue and cook for her youngest son, my Uncle Dave, the bachelor. He worked in a sidewalk photo studio on Seventh Street, the kind where you'd put your head through a painted board: as a consequence, most childhood pictures of my sisters and me depict us variously as peacocks, fan dancers, Jolsonesque smoothies, gangsters—everything but children.

The only places downtown where Negroes knew they could sit down to eat were the railroad station and the government cafeterias; even there, my father says, the union was constantly challenging food-service managers who took it upon themselves to designate separate seating areas for blacks. Except for the government buildings, there were few places where colored people were permitted to go to the bathroom. Usually, when one of the black children in the "sit-downs"—which is what we called the demonstrations of those summers—had to go to the bathroom, we would go running to the

National Gallery of Art, which was about five blocks away. But more often than not it would be too late by the time we got there, and the children would cry, and sometimes their mothers and even their fathers would, too. Years later, when I was a reporter covering civil-rights marches in the South, I couldn't get out of my head a picture of those little children holding their legs together and the pain in their faces. I think one of the reasons I hated going downtown those Saturdays and Thursdays, the big shopping days, was the knowledge that my friends were going to pee in their pants. There seemed to me two cruelties: the indignity of segregation, and the shame our demonstrations inflicted on my friends.

Once, before marching into the streets, Mary Church Terrell, a bent woman with a cane and white hair and a whispery voice, came to talk to the children about what we were doing. When she was a girl, right after the Civil War, she told us, she had been allowed to eat in the restaurants downtown. But that was eighty years earlier, during Reconstruction; it was the last time. If others were to join our cause, we had to be sturdy and be models of decorum—and here she looked at the Negro children—lest we "disgrace the race." Those were her actual words, my mother remembers them, too. It seemed to me she was asking an awful lot.

I have only vague recollections of encountering hostility from white patrons and restaurant workers and downtown shoppers who watched us those summers; occasionally someone would spit or call us nigger lovers. Much more the impression is of curiosity, especially in the earliest days.

Leaving the little law office of Forer and Rein, we would go usually in groups of four or five, black and white. While the grown-ups talked to the hostess or manager—a process that could take considerable time while matters of law, the Constitution, and custom were quietly discussed—we held each other's hands, aware of the stares and the attention. A couple of times photographers from the newspapers, with big square cameras and popping flashbulbs, took our picture. I worried about what my friends in the neighborhood would think if they knew what I was doing. It was one thing to say I didn't believe it was right when they used the word "nigger"; but this was something else again.

A lot of times the restaurant managers announced that they felt *sad* about not being able to serve us, but that it would be bad for business; some said they would welcome a decision in the courts requiring all restaurants to serve everybody. A few times we were taken to tables and seated. Usually not. That was in the restaurants —"lunchrooms," as the local terminology had it. But the real focus of the campaign became the lunch *counters*, in the dime stores on F Street and in the big department stores. By the end of the first summer there were often more than a hundred of us testing and picketing and sitting down every Thursday and Saturday. My mother kept long lists of names, and on the days when we didn't go downtown she'd be on the phone, lining people up.

"Everybody brought their children," she remembers. "God, it was hot as hell."

The dime stores had huge double doors on both sides of their display windows and, just inside, big rotating floor fans. Entering, I would try to delay the proceedings by lingering inside the doorway, savoring the breeze. The lunch counters extended from the front of each store to the back—first the stand-up portion near the entrance, then a long row of swivel seats that stretched to the back. The seats were for whites only. We would walk inside, six or eight or ten to a group, black and white, choosing a moment when there were empty seats because, Annie Stein had said, that meant if we weren't served we would be hurting business by continuing to occupy them. I liked swiveling in the seats. They were made of wood with chrome on the back, the kind that gave a little when you leaned back. The women behind the counter wore hairnets and were very polite, even though they said they could not serve us. No matter how many times we sat down there was always present the element of astonishment, not so much from the whites as from the Negroes who would be standing in the front, packed three and four deep while they ate. They stopped. Put down their hot dogs. Stared. Nobody had ever done this before. The only downtown lunch counter where Negroes had sat in this century was at Union Station. It was said that while the station was being built Teddy Roosevelt heard it was to have separate waiting rooms and a Jim Crow restaurant. Furious, he sent orders to the project manager from the White House saying if the station wasn't built with facilities to be shared by blacks and whites there would be no station. Ever since, the concessionaires had honored TR's dictum.

But nowhere else. Once, on a picket line at Kresge's, Annie Stein handed me a sign to carry: "Is it right / If you're not white / You can't sit down / To eat a bite." My black friend, Tommy Richardson's son Earl, was given a sign saying: "It's Our Ambition / To Eat at Kresge's / In a Sitting Position."

Chapter 10

I cannot say precisely how old I was when the Rosenbergs became a presence in our house. Six or seven, maybe eight. At first they were just a name, the subject of dinner-table conversation between my parents. There were a series of names actually: Emanuel Bloch, Helen Sobell, Ethel Weichbrod, Michael and Robbie, others. Over the next couple of years some of the names became faces and everything became terrifyingly real. Bloch was the Rosenbergs' lawyer; he and Morton Sobell's wife, Helen, came to visit us. Sobell had been convicted with the Rosenbergs. My mother and her friend Ethel Weichbrod organized the Washington Committee to Secure Justice for Julius and Ethel Rosenberg.

There was no national defense committee yet, just a New York movement and a lot of stories in *The National Guardian* which my mother clipped and had reproduced on blue paper with a union bug in the right-hand corner. She spent whole days on the telephone, working her way down lists. Then there was a big party on New Year's Eve; I watched it from the steps in my pajamas. Bob Condon, a congressman from California, my father's close friend from San

Francisco days, tended bar. Abe Bloom made a speech—Truman, J. Edgar Hoover, the Cold War, "this monstrous frame-up," I remember him saying. It was very hot, people were packed into our living room on Chesapeake Street. When Abe finished, somebody passed a hat around. The next morning my mother said that six hundred dollars had been raised.

The money was used to open an office in Inspiration House, on Kalorama Road. My mother helped run it.

I would go with her sometimes that summer. I've never seen my mother more at ease than when she was at work in that office. It was a single room, maybe fifteen by twenty feet, bare except for an old government-surplus desk, a file cabinet, a few bookshelves, and some wooden swivel chairs. My mother usually arrived before the other women, who came in part time. She'd make a list of what had to be done that day, talk with the New York office, call the printer, enter expenses into a ledger. She kept her nails short enough to type, and I thought there was something magical about the way she could move her fingers on the keyboard with incredible speed and carry on a conversation with me at the same time. It was my responsibility to stuff envelopes, fetch coffee, unpack cartons of literature sent from New York, and insert mimeographed appeals for funds into copies of the Book.

The Book was a paperback, blue cover with black lettering. *Death House Letters of Julius and Ethel Rosenberg.* Robbie and Michael Rosenberg were pictured on the back. Many of the letters, my mother explained to me, were written to Michael and Robbie from Sing Sing. Michael was my age; Robbie was three years younger, the same age as my sister Mary. In the picture Michael's arm encircled Robbie—two boys, very much alone, totally vulnerable. For some reason I always identified with Robbie, though he was the younger, the object of his older brother's protection in that picture. Perhaps someone had suggested that Robbie and I looked somewhat alike; perhaps I had thought it. Even today when I look at that picture, it evokes grief—not fear as it did then, but a sense of utter helplessness.

In the front of that same book is a picture of Julius and Ethel Rosenberg, and I can remember staring at it as a child. Her round, rather pretty face is separated from his by a wire screen; he is looking toward her through the mesh. Both of them are wearing overcoats. Hers has a lamb's-wool collar. The overcoats always led me to imagine that the picture had been taken in some sort of van that was hauling them off to Sing Sing or wherever they were taken the night they were arrested, although it occurs to me now that it could have been taken during the trial, maybe in a prisoner's waiting room at the courthouse, perhaps at the arraignment. She looks so gentle in that photograph, gentle and uncomprehending and resigned— and *Jewish*. Hers was a face I felt curiouly drawn to, and to this day my vision of a Jewish Madonna is that face. He looks equally Jewish, his long face framed by rimless Army-issue-type spectacles, the kind that can transform almost any Semitic face into a revolutionist's when worn above a mustache: the classic portrait of the Jewish aesthete, that face, not at all like my father's but the face of any number of men who had been in our house—friends. The Rosenbergs were *familiar*. To a child the connection was unavoidable: if they could be executed, what was to prevent the execution of one's own parents, particularly one's own mother? The Rosenbergs had been married on June 18, 1939, the same day as my mother and father.

There is a poem, by Ethel Rosenberg, "If We Die," on the first page of the book, and I can recall asking my mother to explain its lines to me: "Mourn no more my sons, no more; why the lies and smears were framed / the tears we shed, the hurt we bore / to all shall be proclaimed."

The Rosenbergs too were *progressive* people—and they were going to die for it; they were going to fry.

My first memory of the White House is from a picket line: the crush of what seemed like thousands of people walking past the iron gates, the signs begging clemency, my mother's hand clasped over mine. There would be many other picket lines for the Rosenbergs. And with each the fear intensified, palpable, physical, suffocating, a feeling that caused me to squeeze my mother's hand so tight that I could feel my knuckles lock.

On the day of the execution, June 19, 1953, we spent most of the afternoon in front of the White House. Thousands and thousands of people, the crowd overflowing into Lafayette Square. The signs and the silence, the only sounds footsteps on the pavement. Pictures of Julius and Ethel Rosenberg and of their sons, solemnly held aloft. A sense of helplessness and doom mitigated only by faith, by some desperate belief that nothing as terrible as this would be permitted to happen, that some law of humanity or the universe would intervene, that clemency would be granted at the last moment. We went back to Inspiration House and waited for the telephone to ring. Several dozen people were there, waiting, waiting. If the phone rang before eight o'clock, it meant that Eisenhower had granted clemency. A radio played. Eight o'clock came and went. Then the phone rang. They were dead. At first people wept quietly. Then everyone in the room was sobbing, wailing, and some people got sick. I remember the man on the radio said that all the lights around Ossining had dimmed when they threw the switch.

I shook and cried uncontrollably that night, can still summon the terror—and the fury at my mother for risking *her* life, the utter despair. She tried to calm me, held me, but I was screaming by then, lost, hysterical. "You wouldn't stop," she remembers. I thought *she* was going to die. "Afterwards we drove back to the White House, just drove by to see how it looked. Everyone was still there . . ." she remembers. And even today, her voice breaks, and the tears roll down her cheeks, and she cannot go on.

She must have sensed then that what she and my father were committed to—that progressive political dream they'd lived together—had become a nightmare.

Chapter 11

The published literature on the subject of my parents is not auspicious. There are three primary sources: *Cumulative Index to Publications of the Committee on Un-American Activities (1938–1954, 1955–60), U.S. House of Representatives; Twenty-one Year Index 1951–1971 to Published Hearings, Studies and Reports of the Subcommittee to Investigate the Administration of the Internal Security Act and Other Internal Security Laws of the Committee on the Judiciary, United States Senate;* and *Congressional Investigations of Communism and Subversive Activities, Summary Index 1918–1956, Compiled by the Senate Committee on Government Operations.*

Not the kind of repository in which to be left to the mercy of history: fleshless, federal-green volumes stamped with the imprimatur of our Government Printing Office. They contain seventeen italicized entries on my mother and father. "Bernstein, Alfred (Al)" appears on page 138 of the Internal Security Committee index, followed by a bewildering series of letters and numerals which must be matched up against the Key to Symbols on pages 1–19. The Key to Symbols is the business end, loaded with the language of the

American Inquisition: a lexicon of treason and subversion and infiltration. *Hearings Relating to Communist Activities in the Defense Area of Baltimore*, Part 1; *Communist Infiltration of Government*, Parts 1–6; and *Communist Political Subversion*, Part 1, all devote a certain amount of attention to the organization of the United Federal Workers of America.

To follow this trail and then venture into the darkness of the FBI files is to apprehend the vile process at work here: how these dossiers lay in the belly of Hoover's Bureau, then were regurgitated by some investigator in the committee staff room, then were spit out as a senator's questions ("How did you get your job with the OPA, Mr. Bernstein, was it some Communist who took you into the OPA?"), before, at last, the whole mass got encrusted between the GPO's green covers and shelved away beneath the great dome of the Library of Congress Reading Room.

The principal entry on my mother, in the HUAC cumulative index, leads to a slim volume, *Hearings Regarding Communism in the District of Columbia*, Part 3, July 14 and 15, 1954, pages 5893–963. Her testimony follows that of Irv Winik, whose daughter Marsha was the first girl I kissed (we were bobbing for apples at the shule). Twelve people testified those two days, eleven of them people known to me since my childhood. My mother and Irv Winik had gone to the shule together as children, too. The twelfth witness was Courtney Evans, acting chief investigator of the Committee on Un-American Activities.

"There isn't any doubt about the fact that there is an active Communist conspiracy right here in our midst, is there?" he was asked by the chairman.

"From the evidence available to us, that is right," he confirmed. And the chairman, Harold H. Velde, a Republican congressman from Illinois, noted, "It is here in the National Capital that the Communist Party can do the most damage to our form of government and to our way of life as far as the attempt of Soviet Russia to overthrow our constitutional form of government is concerned. . . .

The Committee investigators are working day and night, as a matter of fact, to uncover subversion, not only here in the District, but all over the country." Then he added, "We just don't have the time to go into all of the details of the subversion here, as we don't have the time to go into all the details of subversion elsewhere."

My mother testified for four minutes. Joe Forer sat at her left. A few minutes earlier, as Ray Pinkson (the electrician) invoked the Fifth Amendment in response to questions about his subscription to "The Washington Bookshopper" (it was on the Attorney General's list of subversive organizations and publications; the bookshop sold left-wing books—and nonpolitical ones too—cheap), Joe Forer asked that the photographers not take any more pictures. He was supported by Representative Francis Walter, who agreed that it was disconcerting to the witness and that the photographers should limit their picture-taking to the swearing-in.

"Joe, how many times have you appeared before this committee representing witnesses?" the chairman interjected. "Have you ever represented a witness before this committee when we have obtained any information whatsoever from that witness on subversive activities?"

"I don't know what information, but I have represented witnesses who have answered all the committee's questions, yes. Quite a while ago," said Joe. "I remember a couple of them."

His request was denied. "News photographers have a perfect right, especially in cases where the witness refuses to give any information, a perfect right to take their pictures at any time during the proceedings," the chairman ruled. He added, "That is a disgrace, asking this committee to hamstring the press."

Another member suggested that Ray Pinkson, a naturalized citizen, be denaturalized and deported.

And finally a colleague addressed the general subject of Joe Forer's clients: "If I had my way, and we had any power, they would

97

really have been punished by putting them in the dungeon." He told Joe, "Your witnesses haven't improved any in time, because they have refused to answer."

My mother was no improvement. The photographers had a field day, judging from the papers. Her picture made the front page of the *Daily News,* the *Evening Star* and the newly combined *Post* and *Times-Herald*—all the Washington papers. A couple of times the committee members asked her to keep her voice up.

They inquired first about her employment, lingering at the War Department.

"Did that employment begin about 1938?"

"Yes."

"How long did it continue?"

"Until 1942."

"Did you work in any capacity for the government or any government agency after leaving the War Department?"

"No, sir."

"At the time you left the War Department, in what branch of the department were you working?"

"The Engineer Corps, Construction Division."

They did not ask if she had applied for a job with the FBI in 1937.

"Why did you do that?" I had asked her at poolside that afternoon in Florida.

"I needed a job," she said. "There was an FBI agent who lived in the Chalfonte who went to the tailor shop and knew us. So one day he said why didn't I apply where he worked and he would send it through. So I did." Then, triumphant-indignant, my mother said, "How do you like that business about being turned down because I wouldn't be subject to discipline?" My mother is not without traces of vanity. "I think I figured out what the reference to my appearance was," she added. "It was anti-Semitic: it meant I was Jewish."

98

At no point in all 2,500 pages of their files is there a single word about any remotely subversive activity, about any suggestion of disloyalty to the country, about any instruction from Moscow, from the CP, etc. Both volumes are really catalogues of associations and movements, seemingly designed to compile a dossier, not to learn anything about the real nature of their activities. At no point is a Communist Party meeting described; there is nothing about the plans of the Communist Party; indeed, very little has to do with the Communist Party except that the subjects have been accused of membership, and therefore their every movement will be scrutinized. The files never say what went on at a meeting to support this cause or that (though agents were present)—only that certain people gathered in Inspiration House, or wherever. Occasionally, if it is really a big public meeting, they will note that the hat was passed and that my mother or father contributed, or that someone was the speaker, but not much more than that.

"Why did you join the Party?" I asked her by the pool in Miami.

"By the time we joined it was just something you did," she replied. "In San Francisco we kept saying no for a time. Badger, badger, badger. San Francisco was militant, active. And joining the Party took on a different kind of meaning. It was about the war the USSR was fighting, among other things."

"What other things?"

"Things you stood for: antifascism; the labor movement; rights for black people."

What did you do in the Party?

"In San Francisco I went to ten or twenty meetings altogether. I don't even remember who was there. Usually there were discussions about how to sell the *Worker*, about the Party line, that kind of thing. The only thing I did outside that was Party-related, formally, was the Committee on Free Elections. I was given money and asked to

99

set up a stand. And I was terrible at it. I'm no good at proselytizing. The committee was trying to turn voters against a proposed law to keep minority parties off the ballot in California."

That was all?

"In San Francisco, my activities were basically work-related, not Party-related. In the FBI file they had it exactly: I worked at the *Labor Herald*, at ILWU Local 10, Harry Bridges' local. Now, that was exciting. It was down on the docks, and the longshoremen would come in and pay their dues and say, 'And here's a dollar for Harry.' Then I worked for the Scalers' Union—the guys who took the barnacles off the boats. All those jobs were through friends, not the Party."

And in Washington? What did you do in the Party there?

"In Washington I was in the Party but not active. I guess I was transferred to the underground because of Dad's position in the union. I didn't do anything in D.C. in the Party, but I sure as hell knew that informer, Mary Stalcup.

"In fact I *was* very active politically: in the United Office and Professional Workers of America, which I'd joined on the Coast, and the Ladies' Auxiliary of the Federal Workers. All three organizations were fighting for the same thing, so they were sometimes interchangeable in my mind: UOPWA, the CP, UFW."

She became involved in the sixty-cent-meat campaign run by the auxiliary of the union. This was in 1946; the postwar price of meat had risen to more than $1.50 a pound, out of the range most Washingtonians could afford. "We sat in front of the grocery stores and asked people not to buy meat, and within three weeks or so we had the price of meat down to sixty cents. It was a real consumer movement. And it worked." Until her appearance before the Un-American Committee she stayed active: in the Committee to Enforce the 1872 Laws, in the campaign to desegregate the swimming pools, in the Rosenberg Committee, in organizing women through the union.

"You should grasp the idea that these people had a huge effect on this city," she said. And, to me, proudly, she named names. She

100

didn't say who was a member of the Party and who wasn't. "It didn't matter."

"Now, were you at any time transferred to an underground group of the Communist Party in Washington?" she was asked under oath.

"I refuse to answer on the basis of the privilege afforded me by the Fifth Amendment not to be a witness against myself."

"Will you tell the committee, please, whether you have any knowledge of the Communist Party plan and how it functioned in the situation where a wife's husband is employed by the Government?"

"I refuse to answer for the reasons I gave before."

"Witness, I know you are here because I can see you, but I sure can't hear you."

"I am sorry, sir. Is that better?"

"Yes, if you will keep it up just a little bit. There is a tendency of all witnesses to let their voices trail off."

And so it went. She was read the informer's testimony:

> Sylvia Bernstein was a member of the white collar section of the Communist Political Association and when her husband returned from the service, she was transferred to the underground club of the Communist Party . . . He was an official previous to that in the United Federal Workers of America, which is now the United Public Workers of America. When he returned from the service, Elizabeth Searle, who was then chairman of the Communist Party in Washington D.C. told me to get in touch with Sylvia Bernstein and inform her she was to be transferred to this underground club because it was dangerous to her husband's position for her to be in the white collar section of the party, so because of this I called Sylvia Bernstein and she informed me that she had already been picked up by the underground club.

"Now, is that testimony true or is it false with regard to you?"

"I refuse to answer for the same grounds I gave before."

101

"You are unwilling to tell this committee, on the ground that to do so might tend to incriminate you, what part, if any, you had to play in the underground work of the Communist Party in Washington, is that what I understand?"

"Yes."

"Were you a member of the Communist Political Association in 1944 and 1945?"

"I refuse to answer on the same grounds I gave before."

"Are you now, I would like to ask you, are you now a member of the Communist Party?"

"I refuse to answer on the same grounds."

"Have you ever been a member of the Communist Party?"

"I refuse to answer on the same grounds."

"I have no further questions, Mr. Chairman."

"Why didn't you quit?" I asked her.

"It would have been an act of rejection. I would have been disloyal."

Chapter 12

The morning of my mother's testimony I went to the playground at school, Janney Elementary, to the day camp run by the D.C. Recreation Department. I was looking forward to it because we were learning to make lanyards out of gimp, doing the box stitch, yellow and black. The counselors wore lanyards, solid white, both the cross stitch and the box stitch, with silver whistles attached to hooks at the bottom. My counselor was Mitch Litman, whom I still see around town now and then; he owns a sporting-goods store.

In the afternoon, I went to lunch at the Gilberts' house—it was sort of my second home. The Gilberts were the one family in our neighborhood with whom my parents felt a particular kinship, a sense of shared values. At the Gilberts' dinner table, as at ours, adult talk was likely to touch on the issues of the day—stated in terms understandable to children. The larger concerns of the Gilberts seemed not unlike those of the Bernsteins. Aside from our house, theirs was the only one in the neighborhood in which I can ever remember seeing black friends. Ian Gilbert was a year older than I, Amy Gilbert a year younger. We were nearly inseparable.

Ben Gilbert, their father, was very successful and important, I knew —the city editor of the *Washington Post*—and he was passionate about the town and its neighborhoods and its people in a way that seemed quite different from anyone else I'd met. I marveled at the license plate on his car: number 490, the same every year. He was also the only man I had ever known who wore bow ties, which only added to how awkward he looked. Everything about Ben seemed awkward: he peered at the world through round tortoise shell spectacles, puckered his lips at the beginning of his sentences, walked with a gait that was really a lope, flailed his arms to make the simplest point.

I saw a lot more of his wife, Maurine, than I did of Ben, because he didn't get home from the paper until late. Sometimes, when I spent the night there, the next morning's *Post* would be dropped off on the doorstep at 8 or 9 P.M., which seemed to me more amazing even than the Gilbert license plates. The Gilberts ran what passed for a truly "modern" household in those days; Maurine wore exotic form-fitted "earth" shoes that laced up the side, Ben listened to long-playing records on the first high-fidelity phonograph I ever heard, and an architect had been hired to redesign and enlarge their house.

Ian was even more awkward than his father—if such a thing were possible—owing principally to obesity and the fact that he had (or didn't have, as was too often the case) a glass eye. "Ian, for God's sake put in your eye before you leave this house," Maurine would have to remind him. Ian, though forgetful, was brilliant, and, to hone his considerable gift for geography and astronomy, he had his own membership in the National Geographic Society. The membership brought with it more than a few atlases and maps of the heavens, and Ian and I spent hours upstairs in his room studying those charts, plotting expeditions on the seas and to the stars. Ian also had a telescope, the knack of which eluded me but not my one-eyed friend. And, once, Ben Gilbert got us into the Naval Observatory on Massachusetts Avenue, where we looked through the

104

huge telescope on the roof and were shown the atomic clock to which all the country's time was attuned.

My memories of Amy are less precise: a pretty girl, blondish, not at all awkward. I taught her how to ride a two-wheeler, played Fish and Old Maid and War with her in the Gilbert library. That afternoon, as we often did on hot, humid days, the three of us set up a lemonade stand at the top of Grant Road.

I had dinner that night at the Gilberts'. I have no memory of the next day's *Post* arriving there; perhaps I had gone home by then, because I'm sure I would have looked at the paper—to get the afternoon baseball scores.

I did not see the paper at home the next morning.

A photocopy of page one is in front of me as I type, the lead story ("Red Party 'Hard Core' in Capital, Velde Says") set off by six one-column head shots laid out in rows of three. "Six More District Witnesses Refuse to Answer Before Un-American Probe," says the subhead. The name of each of the witnesses appears under the appropriate picture. My mother is in column four, looking out blankly toward the right-hand edge of the page. "Invoke Fifth Amendment to duck questions put by House Un-American Activities Group," says the caption.

According to the story, the hearings "were intended to develop" the testimony of Mary Stalcup Markward, "former FBI undercover agent."

The suggestion of espionage hung over the story like the asphyxiating cloud of the epoch itself:

> Indicating the investigation of District Communists may be stepped up, [Chairman] Velde concluded two days of hearings in which 11 stubborn witnesses refused to answer questions about their alleged Communist activities. Six more witnesses, including two wartime employees of the Navy yards, appeared before the Committee yesterday. Like the five who preceded them Wednesday, they invoked the Fifth Amendment to duck all questions about Communist activities.

105

Ray Pinkson got the most attention.

> Well-groomed and dapper, wearing a red zinnia in his lapel, Pinkson proved to be the most arrogant of the witnesses. At one point he strongly objected to the way a question was worded. When the question was rephrased to his satisfaction, he said firmly, "I refuse to answer under the privileges granted me by the Fifth Amendment."

The story added: "He admitted visiting Europe for four months in 1939 and spending four weeks in Russia."

My mother was the last person listed, in a reference to "other witnesses." She was merely identified: "Sylvia Bernstein, a 38-year-old housewife, of 4230 Chesapeake Street N.W."

The final paragraph was about Bill Michnick. The story said that he

> startled the committee when he declared that a Communist can sign a loyalty oath in good faith. The former music teacher admitted signing a loyalty certificate, required of Maryland teachers under the Ober law in 1949. Michnick explained, however, that he does not consider the Communist Party subversive. The committee members wondered, then, why he refused to answer questions.

I remember Bill and Helen Michnick coming to our house when he lost his teaching job. My mother said he had become a piano tuner, which for some reason was a concept I had difficulty grasping. To this day, if I am at a concert or if I see a reference to piano tuning, I imagine Bill Michnick: struggling to walk, bent over, buckling under the weight of an enormous piano strapped to his back.

Chapter 13

There are five single-spaced pages of notes about what happened in the days after that testimony, all from my visit to Florida. I think it is the only time I ever discussed it with my parents. My father had gone off for a dip in the ocean, despite temperatures in the low sixties and two flags up for the undertow. He swims the sidestroke, a slow, deliberate motion, the same as when we went to the beach when I was little.

"That's why I've been hostile," my mother said as we watched him. "I don't want to go through it again." She hadn't really been hostile, just diffident, in the Danish restaurant the night before. Now some distant thought moved near, and she winced. "Mary was in nursery school at the time I testified, and she got thrown out of the nursery school." Her eyes stayed on my father's figure in the water. "I don't think you understand the depth—the hostility toward people like us. There was one little period—after Watergate —when attitudes opened up; that's gone now," she said. She meant that for a year or two the country had seemed released from its anti-

Communist obsession. There have been periods of détente with the Soviet Union, but never really with the American Left.

I hadn't known about the nursery school.

"Each mother had to be there one morning a week. Charlotte Oram's kid also went there and they just threw us out; it was a preschool co-op under the D.C. Recreation Department. They said we'd contaminate those children. There was one woman," my mother remembered, "very plain and soft, and I thought I ought to call her and see if I could start a movement to keep us in. But it turned out that her husband was a rabid anti-Communist letter writer. That's why Mary went to Georgetown Day School. How do you explain to a child that she can't go to school anymore? So real quick we put her into Georgetown Day at great cost, even though we didn't have the money."

I asked her to recall the day she testified.

"I had a red-and-white hat on, white gloves, and I was scared out of my mind," she said. "But I knew pretty much what to expect from the committee. I was just frightened—and humiliated. Taking the Fifth is humiliating, and those bastards ask you one thing after another for the sake of exposure. That was the real feeling, more than scared."

She had not known what to anticipate afterward. The first time that there had been a lot of publicity as a result of testimony before Congress was my father's appearance before the House Labor and Education Committee, six years earlier, but there hadn't been many repercussions. It was during a strike by the Government Cafeteria Workers; the committee had convened an emergency hearing to investigate Communist influence among the dishwashers and steam-table employees who had set up picket lines outside the federal agencies, and the first edition of the *Washington Daily News* had led with his testimony. But by late afternoon the story had been knocked off page one, and friends had been supportive, especially Maurine Gilbert. "Maurine had been in Grand Rapids with her mother," my mother recalled now. "When she came back, even before she unpacked, she called. It was very important to me."

108

She tried to remember the year—1949, she mistakenly thought, and she struggled to put events into order: the Truman Loyalty Order (1947), my father's appearance during the cafeteria strike (1948), the year the union was expelled from the CIO (1950), the year he bought the laundry (1951), his appearance before Eastland (1951), the Rosenberg execution (1953), her HUAC testimony (1954).

"You should keep a little chronology," she suggested. (Except when I see her behind the counter at the department store or at the stove, I am apt to forget how efficient and ordered she is.) Sitting by the pool, the two of us worked out the chronology, and I wrote it on the inside cover of my notebook. There were actually five summonses to appear before Congress: 1947, 1948, 1951, 1954 and 1955.

My father, dripping wet, joined us. "Never mind the dates," he said. The vehemence in his voice surprised me. "The important thing is that nobody who testified did anything. The important thing was the role of the press—her picture in the paper." He started remembering. "There was that woman down the street, that Jewish woman who lived next door to the Freemans. She sent her kid over to play with Mary every day. And then the daughter told Mary she couldn't play with her because her mother wouldn't let her. This was a *vicious* woman." He paused. "One day the woman came into Bill Hayes's shop in Georgetown—this was after he'd gotten out of the laundry business [and into the Mexican-handcrafts business] —and he threw her out." There was no satisfaction in the way he told it.

As if flipping through the pages in a catalogue, my mother assessed the neighbors: "The Nutters were fine. The Meyers were all good; and the Gianarises were fine; they had to be, they had enough trouble with the newspapers"—for this was around the time that Johnny Gianaris' uncle kept getting arrested for running the numbers game in Washington. In those days the way you found out the daily number was to read the last three digits of the *Daily News* circulation figure on the masthead.

"It was within the family that your mother felt the most impact," my father said.

She remembered walking on Connecticut Avenue and running into Maxine Gerber, her second cousin by marriage, and a daughter. "When they saw me they ducked into a store."

I didn't look at her while she talked.

"My cousin Bea came home from abroad and didn't call. Her husband said it was either him or me. And she chose wrong. That was the most shattering thing—Bea. I got shingles after that. I was sick in bed and cried."

Later she got an invitation to the wedding of Bea's son. "Your father wouldn't go. I wrote saying that Dad would be out of town but that I'd go. Then one day Bea called and said she had to come over. She said that Mike would call off the wedding if we came. So I told her what Dad had said, that he refused to go. And Bea said, 'You know, Mike said to me that he knew Al would never come, that he knew he wasn't going out of town.' "

"Your mother was cut off from the local people she'd lived with all her life." My father seemed to be saying that it was because of the publicity. There is more to it than just the publicity, of course, but he and I share a sensitivity about the press. It is difficult to convey the disorder, the disarray, the unsettledness of that afternoon in Florida.

"My mother to the day she died wanted Bea and me to get back together—it was her fantasy," she said. And of course they did, at my grandmother's funeral. My mother is very forgiving, or perhaps the quality I am speaking of has more to do with her need for affection, comfort, security, and being *willing* to forgive as a means to achieving those things. I've always favored my mother in this respect.

I don't know exactly what she and Bea said to each other after the funeral, on the terrace in Silver Spring, but I could see in that moment that the loss of my grandmother was somehow softened. A few minutes afterward Bea sat down next to me on the couch and

110

we tried to catch up on the previous twenty-three years. I asked about my cousin Nancy, her daughter. "She's very very happy," Bea said. "She's married to Peacock Buick."

There was a haze offshore; on the beach, mist.

"I have a comfortable life right now," my mother was saying. "I finally have a nice kind of anonymity, plus wonderful children. I don't want to go through it again." We were getting ready to go inside.

And again my father voiced his fears. "I feel strongly that you don't want to hurt other people," he said to me. "There's no reason we have to spend our declining years justifying what we did—getting involved in a controversy."

The words left me sad, and angry. "What kind of book do you think I'm going to write?" I was almost shouting. "I'm your son."

To which he replied, "That's the best thing you've said."

As we got up to leave, my mother was still trying to reconstruct the day after her testimony.

"I went to the Giant," she recalled. "I was in the Giant picking out a head of lettuce, and right next to me picking out a head of lettuce was Maurine Gilbert. And she didn't say a word. All of a sudden all contact was just cut off. She just went away. . . ."

I was trying to explain about this to Woodward, in the car, driving out New York Avenue toward Route 50.

"The next day was hell," I said. "Some little fucker on the playground said something to me about my mother being a Communist. And wham, that was it. As good a fight as I ever got into. I just remember being all over the ground with this kid. I didn't know what it was all about."

And at that point, in the car, I couldn't go on and I started to

111

shake and cry. And I couldn't stop until I had taken a lot of deep breaths. Woodward had the decency to turn the tape off. And I realized then that a lot more was involved than what had happened that day, or to my parents, or to me as a child.

"And it occurred to me, that's probably why I reacted so strongly to . . ." And then the tape trails off: "(UNINTEL)" says the transcript—and there is a gap.

"Okay, now we go back to that day and let's see—you've got to answer a couple of questions. What did you think of Communism?" That is the next coherent sentence on the tape—Woodward speaking.

"Somebody said that your mother was a Communist, you went fucking crazy, right?" I said.

The kid was over by the jungle gym, against the brick wall, by the boys' entrance to the school. I had never been much of a fighter, but now I found myself underneath the jungle gym, pushing sand into his mouth, tearing at his clothes, banging his head against the dirt. More than anything I remember the rage; I cannot remember how it ended, who broke it up.

"Did you go after him because you thought it was false, or because you were worried it was true?" Woodward asked.

I said I didn't know. "I don't think you have any ability to know. I don't know if it was my anger with him, anger with my mother, with my parents, who knows? It just kind of ignited a rod, a flare of fury."

"But the really important part was that you knew what you thought of Communists and you never thought your parents were Communists?"

"No. And in fact that's one of the things about my lack of acceptance at the beginning of the project. I always thought I was looking for some sort of *reason*, that they would say, in the course of doing this book, 'Oh, we were Communists *because*.' And, of course, they never said it."

112

My pet duck was in the backyard when I got home.

Woodward was really interested in the stuff about the duck.

"You had a duck who would follow you to school?"

"Yeah. School was four blocks away. He'd follow me up the first block and I would have to take him back. Peepers the Duck."

"Peepers the duck?"

"He was named after Wally Cox, on television—Mr. Peepers. He'd follow me. All the time."

My mother was in the kitchen. I cried. And she told me that there was a story that day in the paper. And she said that she and my father were people who believed in certain things and that there were people who didn't believe in what they believed in. And that it had to do with things like black people and white people living together, though "colored" was probably the word she used then. I think there was probably something in there about the notion that everybody should be able not to be poor. And maybe something about people in Russia and America being friends. And she said that there were a lot of people who didn't like those ideas, who believed in something else. And that they were angry people, sometimes bad people. . . .

I know it was not quite that simple, of course. But I am very proud of that answer. That afternoon I was supposed to play with Harry Lowe. His parents owned the florist shop on Fessenden Street. In the fall Harry and I used to make a big pile of leaves in River Road, by the curve, and we would bury ourselves underneath. Then when the cars would come around the bend, we would jump up through the leaves and explode. And the drivers would almost have a crash. I think there might have been rocks associated with this game, though I'm really not sure.

In Florida, my mother had said that Harry's mother had shown up that afternoon instead of Harry. "She saw you in front of the house and she said to you, 'Your mother's a Communist' and that you couldn't play with her son."

In truth, I cannot remember Mrs. Lowe saying that to me. My recollection is that his mother had called mine on the telephone and said he wouldn't be coming. By then there was no need to explain to me why. I think that was when I started to get angry at my mother. I don't remember specifically what I said to her, but I do remember the feeling. The feeling was that I wasn't going to be able to lie in the leaves with Harry and throw rocks at the cars. But then it got worse. Because my best friends were really the Gilbert children. And I sensed that the Gilbert kids were out of my life. Forever. And Harry. But that was all.

Chapter 14

Even though I would never be able to hide Ian Gilbert's glass eye again or leap from a pile of leaves with Harry Lowe, life lurched along quite well for a while. Powell and Barbie Hill's mother—they were twins, he, in fact, was Ambrose Powell Hill III, great-grandson of the Confederate general and my great playmate—visited my mother a day or two later. Mrs. Hill was an exceptionally pretty divorcée (as it was phrased then)—the object of considerable pre-pubescent yearning in neighborhood circles. She worked for Naval Intelligence, on Nebraska Avenue around the corner from my Boy Patrol post, and the fact that she was unmarried and lived with Eddie McCarthy, who wore a brace on his leg and drank beer from a can, only deepened her mystery. That night Eddie McCarthy took me and the twins and Frank Coviello to see the Senators play the White Sox in Griffith Stadium. The purpose of Mrs. Hill's visit— while the headlines still were fresh—had been to let my folks know that the friendship between our households wasn't going to be af-fected by what had happened.

That year Bob Porterfield was coming off a twenty-game season, only the fifth Senator pitcher to win twenty games since Walter Johnson had done it in 1925. He won that night, against Billy Pierce.

I was able to lose myself in the splendid world of that neighborhood and my friends and school. I did not question why, at school, I was becoming a patriotic nut. Miss Bull appointed me the class air-raid warden—a position of considerable responsibility, given her inclination to schedule an air-raid drill every three days or so. This was not too many years after the Chinese Communists had crossed the Yalu into Korea, and now the fear seemed centered on whether other Communists might cross the Potomac. At the sound of three warning bells, I moved smartly into position, pulling down the window shades so that shards of glass from the Soviet explosion would not penetrate our bodies, which, within sixty seconds, were huddled under our little desks, hands clasped behind our heads.

Off duty as air-raid warden, I sold U.S. School Savings Stamps—twenty-five cents, fifty cents, or a dollar apiece—that got pasted into booklets with the Statue of Liberty on the cover. By the time the books were filled they'd be straining at their bindings, at which point they were exchanged for twenty-five-dollar bonds—Defense Bonds, they were called now, not War Bonds. I have no memory of my parents saying anything as I sat at the kitchen table those Monday evenings (Monday was Stamp Day at school) and counted my stamps, all red and blue and green, and then the blank squares remaining to reach $18.75—the price of a twenty-five-dollar bond.

I also collected regular stamps, which went into a fat red album I'd bought in Gimbel's stamp department, during a trip to visit my father's cousins in New York. My finest stamps were given to me by Marcus Goldman. Marcus had a wondrous collection, all mint, not a canceled stamp in the lot, kept in black binders that filled the shelves of his study. His specialty was the United States. Lizzie, his wife, would lead me inside and I would seat myself next to him at the long desk. Marcus would be bent low over the pages, his chin almost touching the magnifying glass. "Burgoyne's Campaign, magenta, two cents, 1926," he'd call off to me. "Yorktown Commemorative, dark red, two cents, 1931." And Marcus would reach for another book while he described the battles and marches and expeditions, then lift a stamp delicately with the tweezers and slip it into a glassine envelope for me, mint and pristine. Such beautiful colors, those old American stamps, such a perfect way to learn history.

Marcus was rich, my mother said; he had inherited a great family fortune but had wanted to be a geologist, which is what he had been for the government. My father handled his loyalty case; the Interior Department Loyalty Board was one of the worst, he says. There were more than two hundred loyalty boards in the federal agencies. Marcus was nearing his sixties then—too old to find another job. My cousin Pat says Lizzie and he would take her to a lot of concerts, and David Samols told me at his father's funeral that he still has the stamps that Marcus gave him.

My stamp collection was stolen in the seventh grade—I'd entered it in a school fair in Silver Spring. However, I still have my first-day covers, hundreds of them kept in shoeboxes in a closet, each addressed to me between 1949 and 1958 in light pencil by Mary Grier or Marie Siegrist; Mary had worked at the Navy Department, Marie at the Geological Survey, and my father had won both their cases.

According to the front page of *The New York Times* of September 23, 1948, "eight hundred and eighty-three Federal employees suspected of disloyalty have quit their jobs rather than face trial." Marcus was one of them.

"That left 4,758 open cases of suspected subversives which the FBI turned over to the Civil Service Commission for adjudication by the loyalty boards of the federal departments and agencies," the same story in the *Times* reported.

All this happened in the first eighteen months after Truman's Loyalty Order took effect.

In the same closet as my first-day covers, I recently discovered other artifacts from that period: report cards, a Webelos merit badge from the Cub Scouts, a lifesaving certificate from Camp Airy. I spent three weeks there every summer, beginning when I was eight. Our camp was in Thurmont, Maryland, adjacent to Camp David, where President Eisenhower spent his weekends. I regarded his proximity with enthusiasm. In the 1952 campaign I had been his only supporter in our house, ostentatiously wearing "I Like Ike" and "Ike and Dick" buttons while my parents debated whether to support Stevenson or Vincent Hallinan of the Progressive Party; he was a partner in the law firm where my mother had worked in San Francisco.

My devotion to President Eisenhower had been such that on the night it was reported on television that the armistice had been signed in Korea I took my sisters into the streets banging pots and pans and shouting through the neighborhood, "The war is over, Ike ended the war." I am aware that this is not how the end of the Korean War was universally observed.

The report cards are an interesting glimpse into these years of my life. I'd be extremely proud bringing them home, the boxes in the "Outstanding Progress" column checked in ink, except for handwriting, which was usually marked "Needs improvement." I hadn't remembered that there was also correspondence on each report, a handwritten note to my parents from the teacher, and a note back from my mother.

Mrs. Slye had written about my deteriorating behavior in the fourth grade. That was the school year in which the Rosenbergs were executed and the Un-American Committee announced its hearings into Communism in Washington.

Mrs. Slye did not mention my leading the Pledge of Allegiance or the fervor with which I read the Bible aloud on Wednesday mornings, or how much I enjoyed going to church at St. Columba's Episcopal for optional prayer on Friday. I went where my friends went, and did what they did. We were all particularly keen on earning money and enjoying the fruits of our industry, especially Daisy Air Rifles.

I do not know if my friends kept theirs hidden at home, but certainly I did, and I have no idea how it arrived in the mail unseen,

118

except that perhaps my parents were away. By then my father owned the laundry, which at first saddened me because I liked him being home with me, working at the dining table.

The Daisy Air Rifle was selected from a catalogue sent by the Wolverine Salve people. I did not know then, nor do I know today, exactly what Wolverine Salve was applied to, or for what reason, but I do know that people bought it in enormous quantities, enough to arm a fair part of the children's population of a whole neighborhood with Daisy Air Rifles. Which was the reason that our streets and the alleyways behind our houses were often blackened at night, the lights having been shot out during reconnaissance.

Chapter 15

I loved that neighborhood and the kids in it and our city, which was defined not by the symbols of the national capital but by the places our bikes took us.

Mine was an English racer—not a Rudge or a Raleigh but a real English racer nonetheless, with Sturmey-Archer three-speed gears and hand brakes—bought at the Mount Vernon Cycle shop and lovingly leaned against the Christmas tree that my father and I had brought home from the Lions Club stand on Wisconsin Avenue. In my excitement that Christmas morning I got a little wobbly coming down the big Massachusetts Avenue hill, and a car scraped against me on the bridge across Rock Creek, by the British Embassy. I was thrown off and dazed. I picked myself up, and my bike; we were both scratched. I have no memory of explaining the scar just below the knee to my parents or anyone else, and I still walk a little funny from what happened.

The Capitol and all the federal buildings, foreboding marble temples, were "downtown." Our city was circumscribed by the river, from Great Falls in the northwest, in Maryland, to Roosevelt Island fifteen miles downstream. Rock Creek, the Potomac's great tributary, represented some kind of immutable eastern boundary, beyond which there was no need to go; we did not know then that it was becoming the boundary between black and white Washington, or if we did we perceived it only dimly. During the daytime at least, the black kids seemed to move easily across the frontier. They indulged in most of the same pleasures that we did: swimming at Widewater on the Chesapeake & Ohio Canal, biking on the towpath, fishing off Fletcher's Cove, netting herring in the creek, taunting orangutans at the zoo, but not riding the roller coaster at Glen Echo Amusement Park, or swimming there. Even after the public pools had been integrated, those seemed to be closed most of the time, because of polio. We swam a lot at American University. There were girls there, and music. "Blue Tango" seemed always to be playing, even underwater. Afterward we'd coast down the other side of the big Massachusetts Avenue hill, to Spring Valley, to the shopping center where we earned quarters carrying groceries from the A&P to the parking lot. Mrs. Nixon, the Vice President's wife, shopped at Wagshall's, the fancy-food store on the opposite side of the parking lot, and there would be a lot of excitement when she was around; men in suits carried her bags.

We ran as a pack. In the evening we peddled subscriptions to the *Washington Daily News* for which we received fifty cents apiece. Sundays, we shagged golf balls at the driving range in Chevy Chase, until the bulldozers came and Woodward & Lothrop put up its first suburban store. We sold seeds from the Burpee catalogue: hollyhocks and zinnias and peas and radishes, dispensed in painted packages colored bright with pictures and promises. Mostly the money went for baseball: for cards and gloves and bats and balls, and games at Griffith Stadium. And it paid for Cub Scout badges and handbooks and camping gear, after my mother had found a troop where there would be no difficulty in my belonging; there had been some problem with one of the den mothers, I had heard her say to my father.

By then I could sense the tension in the family. I'd noticed that my grandmother wasn't happy about things. She was even bossier than usual. And I knew my father didn't like working in a laundry, counting laundry tickets every night at the dining table instead of working with the yellow legal pads.

He was looking for other work by then. Abe Flaxer was trying to help him; Abe had gone to work as a house painter after the union folded and he was put on trial. The Supreme Court eventually reversed his contempt-of-Congress conviction—for refusing to turn over the union's membership lists; then he got into fund-raising. A few months afterward Isaac Polikov got a job selling Israel bonds. The same way everybody had got into the laundry business, they went into fund-raising—the next step up the ladder. It was like immigrant struggle.

Then there came a point where it seemed everything was defined by what was happening to my parents. Partly because we moved— on February 14, 1955, a Monday, my eleventh birthday. It was the worst day of my life. Suddenly I didn't have those friends. For my birthday I was given a Brownie box camera, which I took to school that morning, my last in Miss Bull's class. The pictures I took are in a scrapbook, their corners held down by black triangular tabs. On the bottom of each print is the notation "Feb. 55," stamped by the Kodak plant: Sharon Perper, my first real girlfriend, her hair in ringlets (I'd glide with my feet on the handlebars to her house, down the Brandywine Street hill); Powell and Barbie Hill, the twins; Margaret Harrison, who was in the sixth grade (I was in the fifth) and had breasts; Jimmy Nutter, my closest friend. I don't remember anything about that last day of school except turning the gray knob of the camera and looking down through the viewfinder. There are more than sixty pictures in the scrapbook from that day.

The new house was in Silver Spring, in Maryland, a pleasant suburban house. I had seen it under construction; a couple of times we had driven out in the car. But there had been no comprehension

122

of the reality of moving, of what it would actually mean. My parents said the house on Chesapeake Street was too small.

Recently I drove by. I'd been near Kenwood, off River Road, and decided to look at the cherry blossoms there; it was the first time I'd ever seen them from a car, not a bicycle. There are miles of trees, magnificent in their bloom, infinitely more spectacular than the little rim of cherry trees downtown, around the Tidal Basin. Afterward I drove up River Road, past Malcolm Wolf's at the corner of Forty-fourth Street, and stopped at Forty-third and Chesapeake. Except for the garage, the house looked exactly the same, white stucco with a little screened-in porchfront. We'd had a glider there; my sisters and I would swing in it. It creaked. I don't remember being very close to my sisters after that. By the hedge, where I'd parked the car, there was still a path, worn from trying to beat the throw in running bases; people must have continued using it as a walkway. The lady who came outside said she would show me through the house. Upstairs, I paused at the double doors to the linen closet, my secret hiding place, where I'd climb inside and sink into the piles of pillows and sheets. She told me how happy her family had been in the house and asked after my parents. Her daughter had graduated from college and worked now for a radio station in the Midwest, as a reporter, she said. The thing I remembered best about my room was looking out the window over Forty-third Street, to see if Jimmy Nutter was cutting across one of the yards on his way over, or if Coviello and some of the others had started playing ball or if the Hill twins were outside on their stoop, waiting. We had looked for another house in the same neighborhood, but my mother and father had said there was nothing large enough that we could afford. I'd suggested that we move to Spring Valley, it was only a mile away, but we couldn't go there, my mother said, because it was restricted: they didn't let Jews in.

The new house was quite pretty in its way, all glass and redwood in the back, which opened onto Sligo Creek Park. Harvey Road: the whole neighborhood consisted essentially of that single street, a mile long, one hundred houses, 90 percent of the families Jewish. At the end of the street there was a rambling stone-and-teak house that was in the magazines; Rose Kramer, whose father had been in the Workmen's Circle with Uncle Itzel, lived there.

Next door to the Kramers' was the oldest house in Silver Spring, owned by David Scull and his wife, Betty; she was a Lee, of the Virginia and Maryland Lees. Many years later, when Dave Scull was president of the County Council and trying to become governor, he tipped me to some pretty important stories. His wife had been born in the house—it had been built by her great-grandfather, Lincoln's Postmaster General; now it had a swimming pool and a bomb shelter.

I never got over my first day of school in Silver Spring, at Parkside Elementary, across Sligo Creek. It was a so-called "progressive" school, run as an experiment by the County School Board. There was very little in the way of book learning. On the blackboard was New Math. History and social studies were taught with pageants and plays in which the students dressed up in wigs and pretended that they were John Smith or Pocahontas or Barbara Frietchie ("Shoot, if you must, this old gray head, but spare your country's flag," she'd told the Confederate army). She was from Maryland, and on my first morning of school there somebody named Vincent Godfrey Burns, the poet laureate of Maryland, showed up in a cape and spouted patriotic doggerel that linked Mrs. Frietchie's heroics with the men who had been on the 38th parallel. Hers is one of three quotations I remember from that period of my life; I have no facility for that kind of memory. The other two quotes are the first part of Bartolomeo Vanzetti's letter from prison which I must have learned at shule (". . . Our words—our lives—our pains: nothing! The taking of our lives—lives of a good shoemaker and a poor fish peddler—all! That last moment belongs to us—that agony is our triumph."); and counsel Joseph Welch's admonition to Senator Joseph McCarthy, the spring we moved, about decency.

The primary teaching innovation of the Parkside experiment was called a Freedom Card, a piece of cardboard that enabled you to go

124

outside in the afternoon to make a rock garden and work on a soil-erosion project. Inside, hoes and rakes hung on the walls. Basically, I was a city kid who read very well. I could do some arithmetic. Now I found myself in a classroom with hoes and rakes and teachers who handed out Freedom Cards, though not to me. I went from being a great student to a terrible student in days.

I never passed another math course without going through it twice after that year. And I did not earn my Freedom Card at Parkside until late in the sixth grade; it was awarded primarily for decorum. Instead of working outside in the afternoons on soil erosion, I had to stay indoors with a few other students and work on the Walt Disney mural, in the hallway across from the cafeteria. The mural extended from one side of the school to the other and took four months to complete. There are color pictures of it in my scrapbook: Dopey and Happy and Sleepy, Pluto and Donald and Daffy, Mickey and Minnie.

Our new next-door neighbors on the left side were Senator and Mrs. Alan Bible of Nevada and their children. He had taken the Senate seat held by Pat McCarran, the chairman of the Internal Security Committee before Eastland. Instead of his predecessor's committee, Senator Bible, a Democrat, had chosen as his principal assignment the Committee on the District of Columbia, and had become its chairman. That meant he more or less ruled the city of Washington—though he lived in Maryland and came from Reno.

Next door on the right side was Herb Stein, whose son Ben became my first close friend in the neighborhood. Mr. Stein was an economist, in charge of something called the Committee for Economic Development; he had won a big international prize. Ben taught me how to play Ping-Pong, in his basement, and sometimes Mr. Stein would play, and sometimes my father. Dad was good; he'd played a lot in the South Pacific, that and poker, the winnings of which he'd sent to my mother and me, a few thousand dollars, my mother said, which had helped pay for the new house.

The games Ben and I played became tests of strength and will and skill; I was determined to beat him and I did, though not always. Eventually I beat his father.

One day not long after that, Ben came over to my house carrying a huge red book, as big as the unabridged dictionary. It was *Who's Who*, and his father was in it; he was showing me.

Initially I had no consciousness that the differences between me and the kids in the neighborhood had to do with politics. It seemed more economics to me. Right away part of the difference was the country club. After school, in the warm months, most of the boys on Harvey Road played golf and went swimming at Indian Springs. The only person I had known in my whole life who had gone to a country club was my Uncle Morris. He belonged to Norbeck. There were three Jewish country clubs in Montgomery County.

I asked my parents to join one, preferably Indian Springs.

They refused.

They said that it was not just the money but that they didn't believe in it.

The kids on the block, which was what they called Harvey Road, the whole one-mile length of it, were a very tight-knit group. Many of them had grown up together in Washington, far to the east of where we had lived, in the neighborhoods between Fifth Street and Sixteenth Street. Since my mother's day, Washington's Jewish community had been concentrated in that little enclave. Today you can see the imprint of the Star of David under the cross of the black Baptist Church at Sixteenth and Crittenden, and, faintly, over the huge carved doors the Hebrew letters spelling "B'nai Israel." The city's synagogues, in the time of my mother's youth and mine, were usually referred to not by the names of their congregations but by their locations. Sixteenth and Juniper was one of the last ones built in Washington, in 1957, just inside the District of Columbia—

126

Maryland line. From there the inexorable march of Washington's Jews can be charted by the dates on the cornerstones of the suburban synagogues—through Silver Spring and Bethesda in the 1960s and 1970s, and now out to Rockville and beyond the Beltway, across the river and into Virginia. It is largely a tale of flight, from black people, an exodus from the District of Columbia into the promised land of Montgomery County, Maryland; there, our teachers in school told us repeatedly, the population enjoyed the highest per-capita income of any county in the nation, even Westchester, north of New York City.

Chapter 16

To the best of my knowledge, I had never heard the term "Bar Mitzvah" before we moved to Harvey Road. It certainly was never mentioned at the shule. There the conception of Jewishness was a secular one. And that was the tradition of my mother. Her grandmother, Bubba, had left religion behind in Russia and didn't get it again until toward the end, which was why she moved to Fifth and Jefferson, to be within easier walking distance of the synagogue.

My father, always rational, was an atheist by the time he was in college. His religious upbringing had been traditional: His own father was what was known as a "two-day-a-year man," religious in the sense that he observed the High Holidays. The family belonged to a Conservative congregation, called the Hebrew Tabernacle, at 160th Street, in Washington Heights. "Once in a while we'd go to synagogue on a Friday night," my father recalls, but it wasn't really part of the pattern of living. Religion wasn't important. Still, when he was eleven, a tutor in Hebrew started coming to the house; there was never any question but that he would be Bar Mitzvahed. He had no real Jewish education, in terms of history or culture, as my mother had at the shule. "I never had any interest in it, or in a religious life." Dutifully, he continued to go with his parents to services on the High Holidays. And they observed Passover—which we still do in this family, in a fusion of tradition that borrows heavily from the experience of us all: my grandmother's gefilte fish, and her recipe for *tsimmes*, now made by my mother; the Four Questions, read in Hebrew and English by my two sons; my father, answering in English from a Reconstructionist Haggadah he found many years ago, telling of the exodus from Egypt with weight on the text's lessons of freedom and liberation. (As I recall, there was one year when Woodward found the hidden portion of the matzoh as part of the ritual.)

After we moved, I began agitating for a Bar Mitzvah almost immediately. Every boy my age on the block took Hebrew lessons, and the rewards of a religious life, spiritual and material, seemed worthwhile. My parents were opposed. Almost every Friday night and Saturday morning somebody's brother or cousin or best friend was getting Bar Mitzvahed. There would be a huge party afterward, usually in the ballroom at Sixteenth and Crittenden, sometimes at a hotel, or upstairs at the Italian restaurant in the Wheaton Plaza shopping center. The presents, in terms both of numbers and of quality, were staggering: television sets, leatherbound dictionaries and atlases, portable typewriters, Rolls razors from England (though hardly anyone shaved yet), pigskin travel totes, 35-millimeter cameras, indoor-outdoor barometer-thermometers, jeweled tie clasps, and gold pocket watches. And money. Anywhere from one thousand to three thousand dollars in checks and savings bonds, if my friends were to be believed. Thus, beginning with Friday-night Sabbath services and extending through Saturday-midnight breakfast, my weekends were largely occupied by devotion and celebration.

Even on Saturdays when I did not know anybody being Bar Mitzvahed, I often went to services. Returning in the afternoon from synagogue, I would reopen the dispute. "You won't let me do anything. You won't join a country club, you won't let me be Jewish." Sometimes I screamed. And then I wrote my parents a note saying that they were atheistic Jewish Communists and that that was why they didn't want me Bar Mitzvahed.

I hated what I had done—so much that I forgot about it for years, until my Aunt Rose reminded me of it. She had found the note on the mantelpiece and intercepted it. But I had begun saying pretty much the same thing aloud: "You don't want me to be Jewish. This has to do with your politics. And it's not right. And you don't really believe in freedom. It's Communism. . . ."

Instead of a Bar Mitzvah, my father offered a trip across the country. "We'll send you to San Francisco."

"Nothing doing," I said. "I want to be Bar Mitzvahed."

Finally they relented. I was twelve. We joined MCJC, the Montgomery County Jewish Center, and became part of the flock of Rabbi Tzvi Porath, who agreed to forgo the usual requirements of lengthy study in anticipation of a contribution to the building fund. I was signed up with a tutor, in Riggs Park, whom I went to see two evenings a week to learn Hebrew. Of the traditions and philosophy of Judaism I learned nothing, except what I picked up in the synagogue. And I didn't get to San Francisco to see the people my father wanted me to meet until I started on this book.

The articles of my faith were stored next to my bed in a deep-purple velvet case emblazoned with a yellow Star of David: the *Siddur* (prayer book); *tefillen* (phylacteries, like the ones my great-uncle Itzel's ancient father had gone into the basement to put on, wrapping the thongs around his head and attaching the little box to his forehead so it looked like a light on a miner's hat); *tallis* (the prayer shawl that I insisted the maid iron every week); *yarmulke*. This little packet of plush velvet became the symbol of my rebellion: if I knew my parents were having their friends over, I would slip it onto the ledge in the entryway so it could not be missed when the front door opened.

We now owned a '51 Chevy with power glide, gray, with four doors, as the FBI files note. On Sundays my mother would take the wheel, and my sisters and I would be ferried across the South Capitol Street Bridge (the Frederick Douglass Bridge, it has since been named by Congress), to Trenton Terrace. Years later my sister Mary asked my mother whether the Communist Party held its meetings every Sunday at Trenton Terrace, and was that why we went there. I must admit the same thought had crossed my mind. Even today, when I encounter a reference to Communist Party "cells" in those volumes published by the Government Printing Office, I imagine the dining room in Annie Stein's apartment—below ground, bare except for a table and a few chairs, the walls painted institutional green. I still get uncomfortable driving across the South Capitol Street Bridge. No, my mother had said to my sister, with what sounded like equal parts of amusement and chagrin. "We went there to be with friends —just to have a little fun." Or, as my father put it, "We all hobbled together."

Then one Sunday we were bundled into the car in a hurry. The telephone had been ringing a lot. We got into the car so fast that my sister Laura had only one shoe. Recently, she asked me whether I was going to write about that day. She had been eight at the time. "I was barefoot," she said.

We had just about enough money for tolls and gas to New York. Twenty dollars. I remember my mother and father counting in the car. When we got to the Jersey Turnpike we stopped to go inside a restaurant, and Laura started crying because the pavement was cold on her feet. My father carried her. Inside, we didn't have sufficient money to get enough to eat and be sure we'd make all the tolls. My mother went to a pay phone and called the Gellers, collect; they had just moved to New York, to Queens. We would be staying at their house, she said afterward. We would go sight-seeing in New York. It would be fun. She didn't say why we were going to New York, but I knew that this too had something to do with the troubles.

In fact, the phone calls that morning had been from friends, operating a primitive kind of early-warning system. A subpoena server had shown up in Langley Park, at Ethel Weichbrod's, about

131

ten minutes by car from our house. The subpoena commanded her to appear the next day before the House Committee on Un-American Activities, for an unannounced hearing to investigate the Rosenberg Defense Committee.

The geographical cohesiveness of Trenton Terrace was by the mid-1950s starting to regenerate, in the suburbs, in a little development of modern houses in Langley Park, between Silver Spring and the University of Maryland in College Park. The Forers had been the first to move there, then Casey Gurewitz (he had once been married to Helen Sobell), the Paskoffs, others. The alarm had gone out immediately, from Ethel Weichbrod, who had been served. In Silver Spring, our phone rang with reports of the subpoena server's progress. When he got to Tahona Drive on the edge of Langley Park, we lit out.

We arrived at the Gellers'. In Bayside, Queens. It was very noisy because airplanes were landing and taking off from La Guardia Airport. The apartment was tiny, and packing cases were everywhere; the Gellers had been there only a week. There was hardly anyplace to sit and no place for us to sleep but on the floor. There were eight of us in that little place. We all stayed there the first night and I remember our visit fondly. Mark Geller and I played the guitar. Mark has a wonderful voice; we still sing and play when we see each other. In my scrapbook there is a picture of the two of us making music in the midst of all those packing crates in that strange little house.

We stayed in New York for a week, until the Un-American Committee had finished its hearings.

My father and I went to a fleabag hotel somewhere in Queens, the Franklin Park Hotel. For seven nights we slept together in a big double bed, sitting up and talking until late in the night. I think it was the only time I had ever been with him that long, without my mother and sisters. It was the best time.

My Bar Mitzvah came and went. I sat in a chair that resembled a throne, elevated from the congregation, among them the pillars of Washington radicalism, most of them, like my own parents, Jews who weren't religious. I sang my *haftorah* satisfactorily; the Torah I read from was blessed, in Hebrew, by my Uncle Itzel, by Joe Forer, and by my father, each of whom, according to ritual, brought the strands of the *tallis* to his lips and kissed it before touching the corner to the holy scroll itself. At the time my mother said the whole experience was probably more humiliating for my grandfather than for anyone else: his abhorrence of religion was deep, he was fierce in his disbelief, and I could not persuade him even to wear a *tallis* during the ceremony. Yet my memory of the occasion, and indeed the spirit of the entire affair, is quite happy, not just from the point of view of my own satisfaction, but from what I remember as a kind of transition, an easy mixing of my parents and their old friends with our new neighbors, of my Gentile schoolmates and kids from the block, of the disparate elements of my mother's family. Almost all of my cousins were there except Bea—indeed, all of Bea's five brothers and sisters, and her parents, were present.

The reception was held in our living room; Sligo Creek Park was blanketed with snow.

The FBI was across the street, taking down license numbers, which is how they picked up my Uncle Itzel's Dodge. For months afterward they followed him off and on, cataloguing the addresses and doorways where he would linger for a minute or two. They must not have realized that Uncle Itzel, though in his seventies, was still the circulation manager for the *Forvitz*, the *Jewish Daily Forward;* he was still making his rounds, collecting subscription money from those few Yiddish-speaking Jews left in Washington who took the paper.

For my Bar Mitzvah my father gave me the cufflinks he had worn at *his* Bar Mitzvah—a gift from his family: gold, with the initials "A.B." scrolled in script so florid that the letters twined and danced.

Those cufflinks from my father and a ring, also from his boyhood,

133

were both lost. I lost the ring when I was with my grandparents at the beach, and I remember digging frantically at the water's edge, the feel of sand and grit and tiny stones under my fingernails. Even more painful was the feeling of panic when I first realized that it had slipped from my finger.

Chapter 17

My sense of the next three years is of almost constant turbulence, of forces so powerful that everything seemed to be breaking apart. It is possible to discern now the outline of three constant presences: the FBI, the Montgomery County Police Department, and B'nai B'rith.

Social life on Harvey Road revolved around AZA, Aleph Zadik Aleph, the largest Jewish youth organization in the world—a fraternity of sorts, but, unlike the Greek-letter sorority my mother had pledged, this one took its name from the Hebrew alphabet. She had been blackballed—a single vote cast against her after the pledging —and it was this distinction, in fact, the theory that blackballing was injurious or socially disfiguring, that had led the suburban school authorities to decree that students could not belong to Greek-letter sororities or fraternities. AZA (and its sister organization, BBG, from the crypto-English B'nai B'rith Girls) had no such exclusionary policies and, accordingly, thrived in the Maryland suburbs. There were secret AZA handshakes, in which you could feel the pulse of brethren members, a lot of ball games, and a bit of community service work, most of it done at the new Hebrew Home for the Aged—which had moved, gone with the other Jews, from Thirteenth Street and Spring Road, where my great-grandmother's sister Mima had kept her teeth in a jar, to the suburbs, to Rockville, just inside the circumferential Beltway that was then being built to ring the old city.

I ran with two crowds: the Harvey Road kids, whose lives centered around AZA, and other Jewish kids from school who were closer to the fraternity guys from Washington and thought AZA was a bit sissified. Those kids were also closer to the Gentile elite of Montgomery Hills Junior High, enough to be invited occasionally to the Woodside Methodist Church "cotillion," a word that shimmers still with images of crinolines and soft hair, of gold circle pins and the velvet of Johnny Mathis' voice and "Chances Are." They were good poker players as well, far better than I, and my inclusion and acceptance may have had a lot to do with the serious losses I sustained, losses that put me in constant debt—to Lenny Levy and Barry Kalb, who kept my accounts on the last pages of their loose-leaf notebooks. After each game in the school cafeteria the amount due would be scratched out and a new figure entered, rarely diminished, and every few weeks they would make demands for payments. From the top drawer of my mother's dresser, where she kept the silver dollars given her in the years when my grandparents' customers paid in coin, I fed (with gleaming nineteenth-century heads of Liberty) Kalb and Levy's taste for natty clothes—pink shirts with button-down collars, khaki chinos with buckles in the back, from the Young Ivy Shop in the Silver Spring business district.

My first suspension from school came in the eighth grade: for throwing food in the cafeteria, a whole tray, flung in frustration and sudden fright after losing a twenty-five-dollar pot with what had seemed a sure winning hand. The suspension was for three days, after which my mother and I appeared for a conference in the office of Mr. Hitchcock, the principal. He had stubs for fingers on his right hand. I wondered whether he had lost them in the war. There is little else that I can remember from the session, though I have a

136

vague recollection of my mother dabbing at her eyes with a handkerchief. Mostly I kept my eyes on the principal's stubs; they were
the same shape as my father's cigars after he had smoked them way
down. I did not say why I had thrown the tray, that we had been
playing poker.

Weekend nights in seventh and eighth grade were also devoted
largely to card-playing, around pastel-colored bridge tables re-
deemed from the S&H Green Stamp outlet on Colesville Road,
next to the public library. We smoked Kent cigarettes (with Micron-
ite filters), and I don't think we started drinking until the next year,
mostly beer and malt liquor, bought at Morris Miller's on the District line with proof of age forged on driver's licenses we fashioned
on the library's Photofax machine, from permit applications.

Many of my poker-playing friends lived in the subdivided culs-
de-sac off Forest Glen Road, near the suburban annex of Walter
Reed Army Hospital, a colonial refuge of almost tropical foliage and
architecture, all stucco and rattan and bamboo, built as a casino and
resort in the 1890s in a lush glen fed by Rock Creek. There was
something very mysterious about the place, not the least of which
was a pagoda at its center, and elderly officers with walking sticks
were led around the grounds by pretty nurses in starched white hats.
And one day, walking through the glen on my way from school to
an afternoon poker game, I saw Ike being wheeled down one of the
serpentine walkways. He was wearing a magenta dressing gown, a
silken scarf covered his throat, and he waved to the men and women
in uniform who had come outside to see him. Perhaps this was
during the ileitis or after the first heart attack or maybe only a
checkup—the newspaper accounts have him at the main Walter
Reed during the major illnesses, on Sixteenth Street at Alaska Avenue, near Morris Miller's, but my memory of the event is vivid
because of what happened afterward.

It was late fall, around Halloween, there was a chill, and the poker
game lasted until after it grew dark, which meant it must have been
a Friday night. My friends lived in a neighborhood very much like
Harvey Road—a ghetto of new $30,000 and $40,000 homes with

137

three or four bedrooms built on a single floor, and pine-paneled recreation rooms downstairs. Here too this was a time of constant religious partying—of Bar Mitzvahs and, for the girls, confirmations at the Reform temples or, less often, Bat Mitzvahs. Almost every house in the neighborhood had teenagers, except for the house that old Mrs. Neis the anti-Semite lived in, on Admiralty Drive across the street from my Uncle Itzel's brother Sholem, the upholsterer. She pronounced her name "knee-us"—a sad but crazed and vicious old lady, whom we taunted mercilessly. "Come see us, Neeus," we'd scream, and then tread back and forth across her lawn until she appeared behind the glass-and-aluminum storm door, at which point we would begin kicking divots in the grass with our heels. There was a ritual to these encounters, inevitably ending with her screaming "kike" and "dirty little Jews," and us howling and kicking harder at the grass and finally running off.

The idea of going over there after the poker game that night was not mine, but what followed was, encouraged and emboldened by Crazy Joe Moltz. There were six of us altogether. I threw the first rock, which went through the big plate-glass picture window with such force that the drape inside wrapped around itself. There followed a barrage that took out every window at the front of the house; then we ran around the hedge to the back and shattered the whole wall of jalousied shutters that enclosed the rear porch. More than anything else I remember the cold night air, our breath condensing as we panted from excitement and fear; the force with which I threw those rocks; the sound of the glass; and then the old woman's screams.

The judge was named Noyes and he had the reputation of being an enlightened and humane man, not at all like the other judge who sat on the County Juvenile Court and had sent Mike Alehauser, who was in the ninth grade, to Loch Raven for stealing a car and going joyriding. I sat between my mother and father on a wooden bench that reminded me of the front pew at MCJC. The judge wore a robe

138

like Rabbi Porath, but he seemed kindly, concerned, as he asked Detective Pay to describe the events of the night in question.

Detective Sergeant Oliver Pay of the Montgomery County Police Department tucked his hat under his right arm as he was sworn, and then sat down in the witness box. He was something of a celebrity among Silver Spring teenagers.

Two days after Halloween I had been summoned to the principal's office from geography class and introduced to the sergeant, who informed me, tersely, in the hard twang of the southern-Maryland counties, that Joe Moltz's sister had told the whole story, and that this was serious business. I did not doubt him, especially when, after I confessed, the principal said I was to be suspended for a week, though I remember thinking, as I again contemplated the stubs of his fingers, that the connection between a week off from school and the incentive to act citizenly was somewhat elusive. That afternoon I was taken in a police cruiser to the Silver Spring substation and booked as a juvenile—charged with delinquency.

I do not recall whether Joe Moltz and the others were in the courtroom, or whether they had separate hearings or we were all judged together, for my only awareness was of myself, my parents, Judge Noyes, and Officer Pay, not to mention the specter of Mrs. Neis hovering over the proceedings. The police had found her behind a bed, whimpering but physically uninjured. By the time Detective Pay had finished telling the judge about the damage to the house—only a single bathroom window was unbroken—I believed there was little question but that I was headed for Loch Raven, in Baltimore. Just the name of the place, with its connotation of blackness, a black hole for wayward youths (*Gentile* youths until me, I imagined), was terrifying enough, but I had once even seen the place, on my way home from a Senators–Orioles game: the Maryland Training School for Boys at Loch Raven, a great gray stone fortress behind gray stone walls on Cub Hill Road.

I was asked to stand, and in a voice humid with contrition I said that I understood the gravity of what I had done, and that I hoped the judge would take this into account and allow me another chance.

139

That was the general sense of it. It was a little bit act but mostly for real, the acting part coming somewhat easier because of my very real fear, but I must in honesty say there was a part of me that wanted to wring Joe Moltz's sister's neck.

From his elevated pulpit, the judge looked down on me and asked me to consider the *aggression* of what I had done, not just the possibility that a defenseless old woman could have been killed or could have died of a heart attack, but the ugliness of its intent, to shatter her peace of mind. He then started reading from a probation officer's report, but I didn't hear the words, so overcome was I at last with my own feelings of revulsion at myself. We had acted like Nazis, I decided, I had acted like some storm trooper, we had terrorized this old woman; she was older than my Uncle Itzel, than my grandmother even. The next thing I was aware of was the judge saying that I was to make restitution—$1,500 to replace the windows is the figure that sticks in my mind—and be placed on one year's probation.

"I was horrified," my mother said later—more than a quarter of a century later, when I finally got up enough nerve to ask her and my father about that time. "I *am* horrified." We were sitting at the dining table, and my son Max, then seven, put down his soup spoon and looked at me, trying to grasp what had happened.

"How many windows did you break?" he asked, and after I said "A lot," he asked why, and there was really nothing much I could say to him except that I had done something terrible and I hoped he'd never do anything like that.

"We had no idea what to do about it," my mother said to me.

Then I looked at my mother and my father and asked what they had been thinking when they picked me up at the police station that afternoon.

And, simultaneously, they said, "We couldn't understand it coming out of our house."

"Did you have to pay for the windows?" Max asked, and I said yes.

140

Chapter 18

I became very serious about AZA—to the exclusion of almost everything else, schoolwork especially: I was taking a tenth-grade journalism course that year (getting a C finally) and became editor of my
AZA chapter newspaper. Since moving to Harvey Road I had
clutched at almost anything to win acceptance, to regain the security
of Chesapeake Street. (I had even started a Sunday-morning lox-
and-bagel delivery service with Ben Stein.) And now, to some extent, I was able to gain a foothold through AZA—through this little
newspaper, and the position of leadership it afforded.

I also knew that the FBI had been around, to the Cafferty house
four doors from ours. The Cafferty family was the Harvey Road
equivalent of Mrs. Neis, but in this case the anti-Semitism took a
different form; it rode our streets in a lowered and chopped '49
Mercury, painted yellow and black, with glass-pack mufflers that
burped and belched and cracked warning that the next pogrom
would be led not by Cossacks on horseback but by night riders in
V-8 Fords with overhead valves. At the wheel was a sixty-five-year-
old reprobate, the grandfather of the Cafferty clan, a family of rural

origins who for inexplicable reasons had chosen to migrate from someplace down in the Potomac tobacco lands to this particularly thick patch of urban Diaspora.

I am sure that the adjustment called for on the part of the Cafferty children—*grand*children actually, two brothers in their late teens, one with ragged sideburns inching almost to his chin—was every bit as difficult as my own. They were dropouts, set down in this suburban idyl with only the carcasses and rusted innards of half a dozen hardtops and pickups to remind them of home, and the transformation of their sylvan half acre into a junkyard placed them in serious and immediate conflict with the predominant aesthetic of the neighborhood, not to mention its Jewish residents.

It was sometime in winter when the senior Cafferty, rounding the curve where he regularly drove back and forth for the sole purpose of interrupting our late-afternoon football games, stopped his perfectly Simonized vehicle, pushed the button that silently lowered the window on the driver's side, and announced above the sound of the Mercury's mufflers—now purring contentedly—that the FBI had contacted him. He had been enlisted to help send every Communist Jew in the neighborhood back to Russia, he said, back where they belonged—news that was regarded by the others playing two-hand touch as further evidence of his derangement but that I received with a certain chill. Not that I thought our family was going anywhere, but I sensed that tough times might be ahead.

That year I ran for president of the AZA chapter to which we all belonged, Lincoln AZA No. 889. I ran against Jerry Akman, who lived directly across the street, and he won by two or three votes, after a long and high-minded campaign in which the nature of our "community service" work became the central issue. I argued that it was time to go beyond collecting old sweaters and dungarees for donation to the poor—that we should begin to exhibit some sense of "social awareness" and start to participate in the events of the day; I am quoting here from a June 1959 edition of the *Lincoln Torch*, found in the bottom of a box that my mother sent over when she and my father moved from Silver Spring to be nearer their grand-

142

children; they took an apartment on Woodley Place, overlooking Rock Creek Park, directly across the Calvert Street Bridge from the Ontario. (Everybody still calls it the Calvert Street Bridge, even though the City Council, in one of its early acts of limited self-government, renamed it the Duke Ellington Bridge in 1974.)

I had not realized the extent to which I used the *Lincoln Torch* as a manifesto, in between all the columns and articles about our ball games and dances and sweater-collecting. There were sit-ins around much of the South at the time, even in Silver Spring, where the local ice-cream parlor refused to serve blacks, and at the segregated movie theater in Bethesda, and at the amusement park at Glen Echo. And I was writing (a little grandly) that Jewish kids, Jews perhaps more than any other people, belonged in the civil-rights movement. And that was basically my platform the next December, in Richmond, when I ran for regional (from Washington to North Carolina) president of AZA. I won, on the fifth or sixth ballot, over my friend Bruce Fingerhut. The room was overheated, it smelled of sweat, and I had worn a wool suit and a tie, the same one I had been Bar Mitzvahed in, and to understand the drama it is necessary to understand the fanatical commitment to this organization that we all shared. It was like electing a new Pope, with the smoke going up, I supposed. That was how much emotion and purpose and mission we invested in it.

I had not told my parents I was going to run; I was not at all sure they would approve—either of my winning (and thus devoting even less interest to schoolwork) or of their son being president of a religious organization.

We were on our way to North Carolina, to Hendersonville, in the mountains, about a hundred of us aboard the Peach Queen, the old Southern Railroad train that went overnight from Washington to Atlanta, with stops in Alexandria, Richmond, Danville, Chapel Hill, and on down the line. Each year our summer convention was held in a camp high up in the Great Smokies; the train ride was a major part of the attraction: a twelve-hour trip, with six-packs of beer iced in coolers in the vestibules, the lights dimmed in our chartered cars, and sparks flying from the AZA boys necking with the girls from BBG. At 2 A.M. we reached Greensboro, where the train broke down. Uncertainly we stepped onto the platform and filed into the station, toward a corner where we saw people eating. It was the black restaurant. We had not seen the white side of the station. A moment later the door swung open and a cop burst through and said that we couldn't be served, that we had to move to the other side. He was out of breath from running, and his belly heaved over a garrison belt that sagged with canisters and batons and a holstered revolver. We weren't moving, I said—without considering the implications. The policeman seemed confused, and went to a telephone. A few minutes later a large contingent of the Greensboro, North Carolina, police force arrived, threatening to arrest all of us for being in the black waiting room. Again we were told to leave. I said nothing in reply; by then I had had time to consider the situation. To the group, I announced that anybody who didn't want to get arrested should get back on the train. Everybody stayed. And waited. I was shaking. After about an hour the chief of police, or perhaps he was the deputy, moved to the front of his men. At his side was a woman. He identified her as Mrs. Goldstein, said she was very well known in Greensboro, and described her as a Jewish bondswoman. He smiled and thanked her for coming down at that hour in the morning. She told us we were endangering the whole Jewish community of Greensboro and urged us to reboard the train. Again, I said that anybody who didn't want to be arrested should get back on the train. Nobody moved. For the next four hours, the cops just watched, until the train got repaired. Then we reboarded and, triumphant, headed for Hendersonville.

Then, as now, B'nai B'rith was the largest Jewish fraternal organization in the world; many of its members lived in the South. Moral suasion on the question of desegregation was the stated policy of the organization; it was unalterably opposed to what it regarded as "direct action" by its membership. And by the next morning some-

144

one had gone to the national leadership and said something to the effect of "You aren't going to believe what your kids were doing in the train station last night." Or so I was told when we got to Hendersonville. I was summoned before a council of the adult leadership. And I said I thought that we had done a great thing, that we had demonstrated that Jewish youth in the South felt strongly about civil rights. It was a scandal—there really is no other word for it—because B'nai B'rith had assiduously limited its role to passing resolutions and encouraging quiet community work by its Anti-Defamation League. Nothing more.

Chapter 19

This summary has been prepared for use at the seat of government and may contain information not suitable for dissemination.

Subject has an interest in laundry equipment and sells laundry supplies in the Washington, D.C. area. He resides at 9340 Harvey Road in Silver Spring, Maryland. Bernstein is also local office manager of the Eleanor Roosevelt Cancer Research Office, 1329 E Street, N.W. Washington D.C. On 9/30/58, an admitted former CP member stated Bernstein was *not* known to him as a Party member during the period 1946–52. The Bernsteins attended functions of the Washington Area Forum [of the Progressive Party] in 1958 and 1959; and are on the current WAF mailing list. In 1959 subject contributed to the Southern Christian Educational Fund and was placed on mailing list of "The Southern Patriot." Active participation reported in Washington Sobell Committee in 1959. Subject is a subscriber to "National Guardian." Acquaintances have been identified with CP movement. Current check of confidential informants revealed no additional information.

Residence and Employment: T-1 advised on February 14, 1955, that the subject, his wife SYLVIA, and their children moved from 4230 Chesapeake Street N.W., to 9340 Harvey Road, Silver Spring Maryland, on that date.

T-1 also advised on March 11, 1955, that AL BERNSTEIN continues to operate the Georgia Avenue Bendix Automatic Laundry located at 3218 Georgia Avenue N.W. T-1 on February 28, 1955, related that the subject, as a sideline to his laundry business, was attempting to get some local firms interested in his proposition of making up bluing in small packages and selling these to local persons who operate automatic washer machines.

A reliable informant has periodically advised that BERNSTEIN had been very active in the affairs of the Progressive Party of D.C. from 1952 to 1954. This activity included being elected to the Board of Directors in 1952.

A reliable informant in 1952, 1953 and 1954 reported that BERNSTEIN in these years attended fifteen meetings of the Committee to Defend Marie Richardson and took an active part in planning its activities.

T-15 advised that on the morning of March 14, 1955, Mrs. MATTIE RICHARDSON entered 711 14th Street, N.W., followed shortly thereafter by AL BERNSTEIN. It is to be noted that JOE FORER maintains a law office at this address. Mrs. MATTIE RICHARDSON is the mother of MARIE RICHARDSON who was indicted on November 29, 1951 by the D.C. Grand Jury for falsely stating on a government employment application that she had never been a member of the CP or any Communist organization when in fact she had been a member of the CP and CPA. MARIE RICHARDSON was on March 7, 1952 found guilty of this violation and sentenced to an aggregate sentence of two years and four months to seven years imprisonment and fined $2,000. The Committee to Defend Marie Richardson is an organization designated subversive by the Attorney General of the United States pursuant to Executive Order 10450.

On 2/9/55 William Michnick was in contact with Al Bernstein concerning the problems regarding his, Michnick's license refusal (FISUR [Field Investigation/Surveillance]). T-4 identified WILLIAM MICHNICK as a current member of the CP in the District of Columbia in February, 1955. MICHNICK, who operates a piano store, buying and selling used pianos, was denied renewal of his license in November, 1954 by the District of Columbia superintendent of licenses on grounds that "his character wasn't good because he was under Communist discipline." Michnick's attorney was given until March 1, 1955 to turn in a supplementary brief in this matter.

On 7/11, 13, 15, 18, 20, and 26, 1955, a FISUR was instituted on Al Bernstein in an effort to determine any unusual contacts or acts of security which could be considered as underground activity.

Sylvia and Al Bernstein were giving a farewell party on 7/16/55 at their residence for Emily and Mark Geller who were moving to NYC. On 7/16/55 automobiles registered to Sol Tabor, Marcus Goldman, William Michnick, William Johnson, David Rein and Meyer Samols were observed parked in the immediate vicinity of the Bernstein residence when the above affair was in progress.

T-[deleted] advised on August 30, 1955 that the informant was of the opinion that AL BERNSTEIN was a member of the Communist Party. This informant was not able to state definitely that Bernstein was a member of the Communist Party, but based his opinion that he was a CP member on the fact that Bernstein was acceptable to and highly regarded by such individuals as Anna and Arthur Stein, whom the informant knew were members. On the evening of October 5, 1955, agents of the FBI observed ARTHUR STEIN, FLORENCE TABOR, IRVING LICHTENSTEIN and SOL TABOR in the home of the Bernsteins at 9340 Harvey Road.

T-7, who has in the past supplied reliable information, advised on January 27, 1956 that Al Bernstein was observed at Olmstead's Restaurant, 1336 G Street, N.W., on January 21, 1956. The infor-

148

mant reported that Bernstein was in attendance at an affair to honor Marcus Goldman's 65th birthday anniversary. In regard to MARCUS GOLDMAN, T-3 advised during late 1953 that GOLDMAN and his wife, ELIZABETH GOLDMAN, were suspected by the informant of being CP members. T-3 stated that the informant's suspicions were based on the knowledge that the Goldmans followed the CP line and talk in the same manner as Party members do. The informant remarked that MARCUS GOLDMAN is known to be one of the heaviest financial contributors to the Communist movement in the Washington, D.C. area.

T-9 advised on Feb. 10, 1956, that the subject subscribed to the *National Guardian* and that this subscription expires in May, 1955 [*sic*].

T-9 further advised on Februàry 10, 1956, that CARL BERNSTEIN, son of the subject, was a pupil of the Washington Children's Jewish School.

T-12, who is in a position to comment on some of the activities in the neighborhood of 9340 Harvey Road, Silver Spring, Maryland, the subject's residence, advised on February 20, 1956, that at approximately 6:10 p.m. on February 20, 1956, the source observed two women and a man alight from an automobile bearing Maryland license plate EJ 82-434 and enter the BERNSTEIN residence. T-12 had previously advised on February 17, 1956, that this car was on February 16, 1956, parked between 8 p.m. and 8:30 p.m. in front of the Bernstein home. The source said that the occupants of this car, a man, woman and child, had entered the BERNSTEIN residence.

Washington Field T-3, an admitted former member and official of the Communist Party (CP) in Washington, D.C., stated on September 30, 1958, that Alfred Bernstein was definitely not a CP member during this period and that he had never attended any

Party functions with Bernstein. DETAILS: AT WASHINGTON, D.C.

WASHINGTON FIELD OFFICE will continue to follow the activities of AL BERNSTEIN in relation to his associations and any CP or related activity.

Chapter 20

According to the FBI, the car in front of the house was registered in the name of Samuel David Beck, 9511 Caroline Avenue, Silver Spring, Maryland. I am sure the child in the front seat was Carla Beck, for we had something of a crush on each other, and it was right around that time that she asked me to be her date for her sister Jane's Sweet Sixteen. It was held in the Palladium Room of the Shoreham Hotel, a dinner dance, and I wore a white evening jacket (rented) and bought Carla a corsage for her wrist. The FBI files catalogue half a dozen or so visits by the Becks, and usually a child was in attendance; I presume T-12 was a member of the Cafferty family on Harvey Road. Between 1956 and 1960, there were more than two hundred surveillances undertaken on my parents—by FBI agents, by wiretap, by neighbors. The pattern is always the same: there is not a single activity substantively described, only the notation that a car belonging to so-and-so showed up or that a meeting was held at such-and-such an address and so-and-so was seen to enter or that somebody was planning to go to somebody else's house or office. Beneath these notations are citations alleging that the individuals observed or overheard were members of the Communist Party or were thought to be; or were known to associate with Communists or persons thought to be; or were active in the Progressive Party or in any one of one hundred organizations on the Attorney General's roster of subversive organizations—outfits supposedly "sympathetic to the aims" of the Communist Party.

"Owning the laundry was a means to an end; gradually I got out of laundry." My father had left the laundry in 1957. He was doing the soap-selling by then—making up packages of bluing—and the laundry-bag thing. He was looking for a real job, in fund-raising. "I thought it would be much more stimulating. I'd always liked organizational work."

We were in my living room, Mom and Dad on the couch, very comfortable together, she with her legs stretched across his, until he complained about his back. That morning I had taken him with me to the chiropractor; we have the same problem, lower-back pain and sciatica, though mine comes from running; his came from a bad seat at an Orioles game, he insists, at the end of the '86 season.

"When the guys on the Hollywood blacklist started to get jobs it made it seem that maybe I could get to do some things, get employment with various organizations." He straightened up. "Until then I couldn't see where to go professionally, from the time when the union broke up. I knew it would be hopeless from the political climate of the times."

The Progressive Party was my father's last major political involvement.

"I was totally out of that," my mother said. "There was no place to go—"

"Until the antiwar movement," my father continued. "With the breakup of the Progressive Party, political life kind of ceased."

People were running scared, I suggested.

"I never ran scared." And his tone, sharp, offended, left no doubt. "What would you be active in? The Lawyers' Guild, if you

152

were a practicing lawyer . . ." There simply had been very little else to be involved in, beyond defending one another.

"We still had the same friends, but the political action pretty much ceased," my mother said. "Because it had all blown up. There was nothing to rally around. There were things like the China Friendship Committee, but that had never been our interest."

"Our activities had always centered around the union, and then I got involved around the Loyalty Order," my father explained. Again.

I asked about the Party: Had it stayed active, did it have an agenda in this period, what were the causes it espoused? I was about to ask how it could have done much of anything after the Twentieth Party Congress, after Khrushchev's denunciation of Stalin, but I never got that far; I could see he was seething.

"What are you writing about us and the Party?" he demanded. "I never had anything to do with the Party." He was shouting. "It was not a part of our lives."

"I know that." Now I too was shouting. The book would make those things clear; I hadn't been asking about *them*. All I had asked was if the Party had persevered, if it had continued to be the fulcrum of radical activity for some people, if—

"The fulcrum was never the Party." And, in his anger, for the first time my father defended the Party: "They weren't governed by anti-Soviet feeling—do you have to be motivated by hatred for the Soviet Union in this country?" And then he went back to "the undue importance you put on it"—the Party.

I'm not sure exactly what I said next, but the tone, weary, frustrated, disgusted with his attitude, conveyed more than the words, which were about trying to understand the role of Party *historically* —seen from the perspective of someone on the left, not because he was or wasn't a member, but because he would have a feel for where the Party fit in the scheme of the period.

My father's agitation by this time was such that my mother was becoming irritated—at him, because she could see the state he was working himself into, this most reasonable of men being so unrea-

153

sonable, and I don't think she's any more used to seeing it than I am. She also found it a bit amusing, even funny. He was clicking the bridge in his mouth by then, the new bridge. I'd sent him finally to a new dentist to rebuild his mouth, the first real infirmity of age. "Al, stop clicking," she shouted, and she looked at me and said, laughing a bit, "You're getting him so *upset*." This display, this test, this filial fencing, was quite unlike anything she'd witnessed, and I think there was a piece of this theater that she quite liked.

I tried rephrasing the question: Forget about the Party in terms of your own life, I said; what about other people, people you knew were in the Party? What were *their* impressions of what the Party was doing in this period? What did they say about—

"I find that a very improper question," my father said. He stood up and started pacing back and forth. "The thing you don't understand is that identifying somebody as having been a Communist has many consequences. And you should avoid them when talking about this historical period."

This is about fear, about public opprobrium, I said, not about principle. And here I exploded: at the left and its unwillingness to deal honestly with history, about its self-destructiveness, about its timidity after forty years, about truth.

"Because that's not the truth," my father said. "You think truth is a CP card. I'll tell you what was worrying all of us. We were so defensive we didn't have time to worry about what the Communist Party was doing. I wasn't thinking about the Communist Party, from 1950 to 1986."

He was exasperated.

Why is it so lethal, this subject? I said. Why has this become a subject for a shrink, not a journalist? Why do you react like this every time I mention that there happened to be a Communist Party in the United States? Why not say you believed joining the Party was the right thing to do at the time and simply explain it? Use the book as an opportunity to give some perspective.

"Because the stigma still pervades," my father responded. "I think it's hopeless to stand up and say what happened. I want to be

154

judged by what I did. The truth is that you and I have had more discussion about me in the Party than all the discussion I've ever had about it in my life." The voice was calmer now. "My whole political life was based on union issues, it wasn't based on what happened in a minority party. It wasn't the key. It was a peripheral thing."

"My feeling was the Party went to hell in a bucket," my mother said. "The CP in the city of Washington never amounted to more than a hill of beans."

"And it had no relationship to the labor movement in D.C.," he said. "In all the loyalty cases nobody from the CP ever tried to get in to see us. Membership in the Party was rarely the issue. But membership in the League against War and Fascism was, for instance, in the earlier period."

Fronts.

"Fronts were run by people sympathetic to certain aims—they had little to do with the CP."

I did not challenge him. I mentioned sitting next to Paul Marston on the Eastern shuttle the day before. My father had liked his column in that Sunday's *Washington Post,* it had unloaded on the Redskins' coaching, in the wild-card game against the Giants. "Tom Marston would be a good case example," he said. "He had a deep feeling for labor stuff. The Library of Congress was a hell of a tough place to work." My father had handled his loyalty case—and won. On the plane Paul had said that his father had never been politically active again, and that he seemed to have changed after that— though the two of them had never discussed what happened. He thought his father had become introverted afterward, had retreated into himself. ("I studied an old picture of him," Paul said. "I had never seen him like he was in that picture—animated, excited.") Both my mother and my father seemed interested in that.

My mother returned to the subject of what happened after the early fifties. "There was nothing that interested me politically." She turned toward him on the couch. "You never even went to a lot of cause meetings when you were active."

"My activity was never that great outside of the union."

And to me she explained, "Some people ate meetings with bread, as we used to say." She added, "The only thing I was active in was the Rosenberg thing."

He ran his hand through his hair—silver-gray, the same color as mine; he'll do that often when he's thinking, recollecting. "My own perception was that with the death of the Progressive Party the people on the left saw very little in the way of any distinctions in the political vessels at their disposal."

On the couch my mother was thumbing through a copy of "The Red Diaper Baby Book," an account of the proceedings of a gathering the summer before of a couple of hundred sons and daughters of American leftists. I had attended, a weekend in a camp in Vermont—looking once again in the wrong place for answers found finally closer to home. The best part had been the singing.

"God, the rhetoric!" my mother said, and closed the book.

Looking back, why had the left died? I asked.

"It was on the defensive. And we should have laid back a little," my father said.

Meaning what?

"Not following the line so much. The dogma. There were too many trolley-car guys. The strength of the left was the unions. When they were broken that was the end."

"There was nothing remaining," my mother said. "The only unions were the AFL. I got involved in the Stevenson campaign."

"Maybe I've learned something," my father was saying. "I went along with the dogma. That was a mistake. I became a religionist and I don't believe in religion."

156

Chapter 21

Koplow stated that Bernstein was just like Bob Condon in that he was a liberal guy who would fight for anybody that got kicked around. . . . On 6/23/54 Condon was observed in the Bernstein residence watching a ballgame on TV. (FISUR)

For years my parents were unaware of the magnitude of the surveillance. Annie Stein had told them that her trashman had warned her he had orders to segregate the Steins' trash and turn it over to a supervisor. And they knew the FBI had gone to George Koplow, a friend, and asked some questions—earlier, before the move to Silver Spring, in 1954, according to the files. But not much else.

[Name deleted] advised that Bernstein devoted practically his entire time to the handling of loyalty cases. [Deleted] has had occasion to ascertain that Bernstein had, with few exceptions, been rather successful in obtaining favorable decisions for members of the UPWA-CIO employed by the Government.

After my father was able to get work, the Bureau regularly questioned his employers, about every six months or so. In 1958 he had gotten his first fund-raising job, with the Eleanor Roosevelt Institute for Cancer Research; in 1960 he went to the Union of American Hebrew Congregations; he was hired by the National Conference of Christians and Jews four years later.

"I was working on Jefferson Place, downtown," my mother said to my father suddenly—we were back in the living room, having coffee—"and I remember telling you that two guys in a car had followed me from Harvey Road to where I worked." That was in 1962, according to the files. "But I really didn't know that they had come around to the neighbors until someone told me Rose Kramer had said something, early in the 1960s. Rose Kramer told people they'd visited her."

"We had good relations with Rose Kramer until the Spelman campaign," my father recalled; he had decided in 1966 to help raise funds for the campaign of a liberal Democrat running for Congress in Montgomery County—his first political activity in years. "Rose told Rita Lagoe that she ought to keep away from us, that we were Communists." Still, he said, "There was no sense of not accepting us in the neighborhood. Our social relationships there weren't very deep, because we moved in our own community."

"We could have formed close friendships had we wanted to," my mother said.

"Mildred Stein never brought it up," my father noted—even later, when Herb Stein had gone to work at the White House, as chairman of President Nixon's Council of Economic Advisers, and Ben Stein was one of the President's speechwriters.

"I never had a problem," said my mother. "Mrs. Bible was always very pleasant. And the Senator always said good morning. Your dad would see him sometimes in Nevada, and that was pleasant, too."

I was sixteen years old, a junior in high school getting Cs and Ds and Fs. The courses I was passing were the ones in which I could

158

take essay exams, because I could write my way through those. That year I had a free fourth period, to work on the school paper; I was the circulation and exchange manager—a job that took no more than ten minutes a day. Then came lunch, devoted largely to smoking cigarettes in the Grove, the wooded front lawn of Montgomery Blair High School, named after the same Postmaster General whose great-granddaughter now owned the neighborhood bomb shelter. Fifth period was study hall. And on many Mondays, Wednesdays, and Fridays I was excused from sixth-period class because I was a regular on *The Milt Grant Show*, a local version of *American Bandstand* (on Tuesdays and Thursdays black kids danced).

I was also a competent pool player, and each afternoon after putting in a few minutes on *Silver Chips*, the school newspaper, I would head for Jim Myers' Silver Spring Recreation Center, the local pool hall, up a darkened flight of steps and above the municipal parking lot on Thayer Avenue. I owned my own stick, a two-piece job that stands now in a corner of my dining room, a fond and suitable memento of that middle period of my teenage years. Occasionally on evenings or weekends Dad would come with me—we'd shoot a few games of pool and then play the pinball machines.

At the time, my parents had not seemed mollified by the fact that my involvement in AZA might move the organization's values in the same direction as their own. Their primary concern was that I was not spending time on my schoolwork. The trip to North Carolina had been sandwiched between two summer-school sessions: the first to repeat Spanish, the second geometry. That year there were endless discussions about failing grades, report cards, about not doing homework—after which I'd obediently go to my room and spend hours inside with the door closed. And for a few months my parents would be hopeful, until the next report card, for in fact I was writing letters those nights, planning trips to spread my particular interpretation of the AZA gospel, corresponding with my fellow Aleph Godols around the country—for that was what presidents of the organization were called, from the Hebrew word for "teacher," *godol.* I had a presidential travel budget of roughly twelve hundred dollars, almost as much as the damage calculated to Mrs. Neis's windows and psyche. It was my plan to run for Grand Aleph Godol the next summer, for president of the whole shebang, but when I finally arrived at Camp Blue Star, in Pennsylvania, in the Poconos, it was clear that I hadn't a prayer; the adults of B'nai B'rith, while not exactly brokering the convention, had steered it toward a debate over whether their Youth Organization should be involving itself in matters outside the mainstream of American Jewish custom and practice; the fundamental question was the same one that had been raised by the Jewish bondswoman in Greensboro: whether a radical agenda might endanger the security—economic and social—of Jews in their communities. Finally a stack of resolutions was passed affirming B'nai B'rith's commitment to civil rights, and I was elected Honorary Grand Aleph Godol, a compromise to which I reluctantly acceded in an emotional ceremony in which I was given a gavel with my name engraved on it, and sent off.

I have some wonderful feelings about that period of my life—a haze of poker and pool and highway and rock and roll. My world was expanding with the mobility (and unaccountability) that came with a driver's license at age sixteen. Many of us had actually started driving earlier, in junior high, sneaking out of our houses at three in the morning (Peter Berman, Richard Freedman, Dick Edelman, and I did this frequently) and pushing one of the family cars out of the driveway, so that our parents couldn't hear it getting started. Then we'd drive around Silver Spring until just before dawn, full of ourselves, until the excruciating moment when a cop pulled up to a light on the other side of the intersection, and whoever was driving had to prop himself up on the front seat and raise his head above the steering wheel.

Released at last at age sixteen from such terrors, we drove out Route 301 to play the slot machines in Waldorf, thirty minutes away in southern Maryland, the only place in the country outside of Nevada where they were legal; the Maryland "casinos" had big floor shows with country music, and on Saturday nights we drove to

160

Baltimore, to The Block, where a favorite stripper, Chili Pepper, would throw her G-string in our direction and go bump in the night.

Fridays there were "socials" at the Silver Spring armory of the Maryland National Guard, or in Prince Georges County, at the Hyattsville armory, big dances, with kids from the District and from the Maryland counties, blacks and whites, Gentiles and Jews. We danced the Queenstown, which the tough girls from Queens Chapel Road in Riggs Park had invented—it had one step less than Philadelphia style, which they did on *Bandstand*.

Today, mostly it is the music that evokes that time. After Buddy Holly's plane went down, with Ritchie Valens and the Big Bopper, we all wore black armbands to school for a week.

The big draw of the socials, aside from the music, was the fights, often between the Italians and the Greeks, which meant that Pete Brascinos, who had polio, would be involved, thus holding out the possibility of an extra measure of savagery, from the use of his metal crutches. But usually, before there was too much blood, a couple of uniformed Montgomery County policemen would wade into the middle of it, and a few minutes later Officer Pay would appear and everybody would decide it was time to go home.

Once, after such a fight I pulled up at the stoplight at Colesville Road and Fenton Street, in front of the Hecht Company department store in the family sedan—a 1958 De Soto, four doors. Maryland license number HL 1762, according to the FBI files, although it was much more distinguishable by its sickly pink-beige color and the fins that grew out of its hindquarters and swept upward like some great pterodactyl. Larry Marine, who owned a '58 Impala convertible, turquoise, with a four-speed shift, was gunning his considerable engine in the next lane, and we lit out in a screech of rubber, heading for the unopened section of the new Beltway, where the real racing was done. I was doing close to ninety when I saw the police cruiser in the rearview mirror, and at that moment Ronnie Oberman, who was in the backseat with a couple of other guys who had been involved in the incident at Mrs. Neis's house, shouted, "Bernstein—he's got a gun out!" And at that point I started to slow down, and I ended up eventually with the car on the lawn of the Maryland–National Capital Park and Planning Commission. Two policemen jumped out of their cruiser and took me out of the De Soto and threw me against it so hard I thought my back was broken.

I was taken to the substation, where Officer Pay booked me, and again I had to go before Judge Noyes, and I lost my license for six months, and was again put on probation, this time for another year.

My father decided that I had to do something—apply whatever energy and skills I had to doing something constructive. A newspaper seemed to him a suitable place to do it. And I had had that journalism course.

He knew a lot of reporters, from when the union had been a major force in the town. There were three Washington papers: the liberal morning *Washington Post* and *Times-Herald*, the conservative afternoon *Star*, and the afternoon tabloid, the *Daily News*. It was unthinkable that I would go to the *Post*: Ben Gilbert was still the city editor, and Jerry Kluttz, who wrote the "Federal Diary" column, had treated the union—and my father—with disdain after the Loyalty Order took effect. My father called Joe Young, the government columnist at the *Star*, who had covered the loyalty issue for the paper.

My picture of a city room will always be the *Washington Star* newsroom. Row after row of steel desks, and typewriters clacking and people yelling, "Copy!" Putting out five editions a day. I thought it was the most exciting thing I'd ever seen. I still do.

It was the spring of 1960. It took me until August to get hired, until I had grown some (I was about 5'3" when I was first interviewed) and had knocked on the head copyboy's door enough for him to realize I wasn't going to go away.

A quarter of a century later I asked my father what had led him to try to get me hired at a newspaper.

He said, "I wanted to get you a summer job. I thought you would find it stimulating."

162

Book Four

Chapter 22

New York, 1987. My father is standing, hands in his pockets, as he reads. He wears a burgundy turtleneck, the same color as the old robe. I watch from my room. He seems purposeful, competent; there is something different about the way he carries himself when he is engaged, there is nothing absentminded about his manner. Boxes are piled on the table—his files, the transcripts from the hearings, everything intact, preserved as if they were still the stuff of his life. That morning he had arrived with a small suitcase and a raincoat. By noon he was reading—Emily Geller's case first. At the seder in April, the same week as his seventy-seventh birthday, I had asked a question about her case. "I can't remember," he said. "I'd have to look at the files."

There is a perception, I know, that the era began with the Un-American Committee, or Joe McCarthy, or Whittaker Chambers in the pumpkin patch. It didn't. Somehow I always understood that it began on those nights in the dining room.

There was a radio-phonograph console against the far wall, from before the war, the kind that opened from the top, with a Gerrard changer inside, and, stacked on the spindle, shellacked 78s; the songs playing were "Viva la Quince Brigada," from the Spanish Civil War, "Let My People Go," sung by Paul Robeson, and "Talking Union" by Pete Seeger.

He knew exactly what he was doing when he came back from the Army: he intended to spend the rest of his working life in the labor movement. There were no doubts, though it meant taking a financial beating. Certainly he did not sense anything dangerous about it or about his past. I remember vividly him coming back (though the psychiatrists say you have to be older to remember such things), him bending over the crib on Argonne Place, in my grandmother's living room. I remember the cap, khaki, three-cornered, and my mother standing behind him, smiling, and him stroking my face. He was at Camp Adair, in Oregon, when I was born, then he shipped out from San Francisco. I was twenty months old when he came home.

"I never had a sense of danger until later—that would come after Truman's reelection. It was really after Truman's reelection that the Loyalty Order went into full force. In '48–'49. The Bailey case really knocked me out. The loss of that case."

This stated at lunch. He had just spilled his coffee, something I have been observing him do for over forty years. He had already read through several hundred pages. I asked him if it was fun; I'm not sure why I chose to use that word. Perhaps because I was so happy to be with him, just the two of us together.

"I try to see where I made my mistakes. I might have been a little too hostile in Emily's case, but it was the only thing I could figure at the time." He rubbed his face. "I didn't have any experience at these kinds of proceedings—nobody did."

And feelings? What was evoked when he held the onionskin between his fingers, read his objections, remembered the hearing room?

"It's a long time ago, Carl." He paused. "When I read the individual cases, however"—and here he moved his hand to his brow,

166

and pushed against it, hard—"especially cases that were lost, then the real horror comes back. People out of work, children ostracized.

"Yeah, uh-huh," he said vaguely when I asked had he ever had a sense of his own children being ostracized. "It's hard to explain to you kids."

I couldn't tell whether he was talking about then or now.

After lunch, walking up East Sixtieth Street, he told me he was being interviewed for a book about the labor movement; it was to include a section on his union, the United Public Workers, and on the expulsion of the left-wing unions from the CIO in 1950. "Everything that happened in Washington, opening up the cafeterias to black people, breaking out of the counting rooms, beginning a consumer movement, hiring black bus drivers in the city, setting up the restaurant picket lines—that was our people." Preparing for his interview had put some things into perspective for him. "We were the conscience of the city." He said it simply, matter-of-factly, it was not intended as a boast. When I visited Annie Stein, in 1978, three years before she died, she gave me a UPW pin to give to him, a lapel pin, which sits in his dresser drawer. I doubt that he has ever worn it; he is not a sentimentalist, at least not outwardly.

Annie had told me about the sit-down in the counting rooms, at the Bureau of Engraving and Printing, where hundreds of black women counted the dollar bills. She had blown a whistle, and the counting of greenbacks ceased until the union had negotiated an agreement with the government that opened up other positions for blacks at the bureau. I especially remember the huge fans whirring in the heat of the counting rooms and how they would make the sheets of uncut bills flutter. In grammar school my two favorite tours in Washington were the Bureau of Engraving and the FBI Building; the G-men took target practice in the basement, and afterward each of us was given one of the targets, full of holes of different calibers in the vicinity of the chest.

That afternoon in my New York apartment my father examined his handwritten notes on Emily's case. They were folded neatly across the middle, removed from a loose-leaf notebook and held together for forty years by a red rubber band. "I forgot how much I wrote." His fingers seemed to me thinner now, and his wedding band slid a little as he turned the pages.

"The basic problem is that you can never cross-examine, because there are no witnesses. The problem is that you don't know what they had in the way of evidence and you're trying to guess."

Emily's case focused on her union activities and people she knew from the union. Among the charges were that she knew Annie Stein. "It was really the leadership of the union—core people—who got the first charges." Emily was secretary of Local 203. Paul Marston's father was a shop steward in the stacks at the Library of Congress. "The most active members were the ones charged." Dorothy Bailey was president of Local 10. "None had a background you or I would call left-wing."

At times my father seemed to be talking more to himself than to me as he read. "Now I remember this crazy bit of illogic. Emily says about forty times in here that she had no connection with the Communist Party." I looked up. "I know of no cases where perjury charges were filed. The best answer to all of these people being subversive is that no perjury charges were brought." Of all the cases in the files, there is none in which the accused took the Fifth Amendment. Pleading the Fifth Amendment in this forum would have been tantamount to a finding of disloyalty.

How had he advised people about perjury, the risk?

"I would let them know that they were under oath. Right away, beginning with the interrogatory."

The interrogatory was the first step. It accompanied the set of charges in the mail and asked the respondent to address each allegation specifically in writing.

"Please note hereon any comments you desire to make regarding your loyalty to the United States that you believe should be considered in determining your suitability for federal employment," the final portion of the interrogatory asked.

168

"I am a loyal American and fully support our form of government," Emily Geller wrote.

DEAR MRS. GELLER:

Reference is made to your transfer, March 29, 1947 to the position of Position Classifier. As part of the process of determining your suitability for Federal Employment, an investigation of you has been conducted under the provisions of Executive Order 9835, which established the Federal Employees Loyalty Program. This investigation disclosed information which it is believed you should have an opportunity to explain or refute. . . .

Information contained in the file shows that on or about April, 1946, as Emily Levin, Lewis, Geller or some other name, you took over as Secretary of the Government Underground Group (or similar name) of the Communist Party and thereafter actively participated in carrying out the duties of this office in furthering the cause of Communism. . . .

The Commission has been informed that in approximately 1942, as Emily Levin, you became a member of the Washington Bookshop Association, that you were a dues paying member from about 1942 through 1946, part of the time under the name of Emily Lewis, and that you participated in the activities of this organization by attending meetings, etc. etc.

Information contained in the files shows you are presently an active member of the Southern Conference for Human Welfare and that you have participated in the activities of this organization by attending meetings, etc. . . .

The Commission has received information that you are or were an active member of a union which over a period of years has been Communist infiltrated and dominated and that you are and have been closely associated with officers and members of this union who are active in or officers in the Communist Party, the Communist Political Association and/or Communist Front organizations. . . .

The Commission has received information that (1) while on duty as a Classification Analyst and Classification and Personnel Officer you devoted considerable government time to union activ-

169

ities, (2) in the matter of selection, promotion and upgrading of personnel you showed favoritism to members of one particular union, and (3) you used your official position to infiltrate new members of the Communist Party into the government service and into the Underground Group of the Communist Party. . . .

Information contained in the file shows that over a period of years you have resided with, associated with and been in contact with known and admitted members of the Communist Party, the Communist Political Association and Communist Front organizations.

Emily Geller: You remember how hot it is in Washington in August, Carl. We were living on Joliet Street—this was 1948. There had been a few weeks of activity around the Henry Wallace campaign for president, which was terribly exciting; we had a big dinner, and Wallace came. There was a wonderful feeling of excitement that summer; great artists, people of stature were supporting him. I distinctly remember on one hand having a very good feeling about the summer and that terrible feeling of this thing coming.

The union had been fighting the Loyalty Order and talking about it. So you began to feel this heating up, some of the fear of the executive order. But as I remember it, except for the fact that I had a job in Personnel and there weren't many people in the union in Personnel, there was nothing to distinguish me; I never had a left-wing background. But neither did Dorothy Bailey, whose case was right after mine. There was no rhyme or reason to it, that was what was so crazy. We knew it was going to happen, but we didn't know to whom it was going to happen, in what order. Because with the anonymous informants somebody would say something about somebody and you never knew whom it was going to hit.

There was a receipt saying Registered Mail, go to the Post Office. I don't remember going, but I can still see the letter. When I opened it I had that feeling in the pit of my stomach that you know something terrible is going to happen. The first thing was to call the union. They said see Al Bernstein. I didn't know him. I had met him once.

That night we drove to the Progressive Party convention in Philadelphia and for a few moments there was this wonderful feeling of maybe the world was going to be okay. I remember Lillian Hellman, Rockwell Kent, Louis

170

Untermeyer and all the great names. They had this broadcast the night before, all these idols, great literary idols who came out for Wallace, and the wonderful speeches, and Pete Seeger. I remember the Young Progressives coming up and asking us to join and thinking, Isn't that wonderful, they think we're twenty-one or something. I was twenty-eight. You know, that wonderful high feeling. And then coming back to Washington and feeling uhhhhh-oh, that awful business, you know, that I had to face.

We came back Sunday, and Monday night we had an appointment to go to your house, on Chesapeake Street. We didn't know many people who had houses, because we were the young group in the union, you know. Your father was ten years our senior, he was thirty-eight, a family man, had children. Your mother was pregnant with Laura, she was huge, she could practically not move she was so big. It was beastly hot, as only Washington can be. Your house was, to put it mildly, a mess. There was a hole in the ceiling.

I remember your mother's smile, how warm she was. Your mother sat in with your father. It was not, you know, that your mother would be banished to another room. I didn't know your father, but he was God to me—I was terrified, and not knowing what to say.

The only way to describe it is like when you go to a doctor and you don't know what's going to happen, you think he's going to solve all your problems. I don't remember exactly what was said. I remember the kindness and the warmth, that he would be able to take care of this. It was the feeling of coming to somebody who was saying, "You know, we'll take care of it, we're here, we're here for you."

Mark Geller: I didn't think that this man was going to take care of everything. He was just a man. He seemed to me to be a competent person, but I knew that the world was a lot bigger than Al Bernstein and us, that the issues were a lot bigger, that he was going to do the best job he could, but where we would end up I had no idea.

When the executive order came out, what it indicated to me at any rate was that this was part of the general onslaught against progressive people. It began with the government workers, and in no time flat it had moved

171

across the country. After the government workers, pretty soon it was workers in defense industries, pretty soon it was workers all over the country, the Hollywood Ten, that they shut down. It was the first really McCarthyite act after World War Two in America.

I never was a Communist Party member but I was charged with disloyalty. You have to understand everything against the background of what was taking place. Otherwise there is absolutely no meaning—except in the context of that period. All these informants and all these charges that don't mean things, et cetera, were really unimportant. What was really important, at least from my point of view, was the fact that the whole thing was a vehicle for driving everybody out of the government, or everybody out of private industry, or everybody who had some idea in mind of trying to inhibit the development of the Cold War.

We were so unimportant really. We were zeros, I mean who the hell were we? We were not in top agency positions. We were ordinary union members. But we had a point of view, on the question of race and the question of unions. You have to remember that Washington was a Southern town; it was Jim Crow including the government. All of the government agencies had separate dining rooms or separate dining areas for blacks and whites. In a sense we were radicals in that we were breaking Southern traditions. And there were some who also came with a point of view of politically coming out of the war and not wanting to see a recurrence of an international debacle. And although we were not important people, still we were there and we were active in these kinds of things. And in a place like Washington, D.C.

Suddenly there were picket lines all over the place. Here came all these people from all parts of the country, particularly New York Jews, to work for the federal government, people from union backgrounds, from the North and the West. They brought their own ideas and there was a lot of conflict. You have to remember that unions in the federal government at that time were not looked upon sympathetically. And suddenly all these people came to town and were breaking up social traditions. And that was a cause of great discomfort, I'm sure.

Everybody who's for equality has to be a Red: that was the attitude. So you get a list of the active members of the union and ipso facto they are

172

Communists. We were the eternal enemy. If you understand that, you understand everything. Everybody in opposition had to be driven out.

Emily's memory is precise: a room with a long desk, a stenotypist. She sat on one side with my father. On the other side sat four people asking questions. She says my father took an aggressive tack and stuck with it, challenging the basis of the allegations throughout. The first hearing lasted a full day. Her husband, Mark, didn't go; nobody could attend except counsel. "Your father, as I remember it, was not treated as you expect a lawyer. I would think that there was some hostility toward your father—a feeling like the way the lawyers were treated in the Hollywood Ten cases. He was suspect, too—because he was handling the case, because he handled loyalty cases. And he was from the union."

The transcripts bear her out.

The charge that could not be adequately addressed, neither proven nor disproven, was whether Emily Geller was a member of the Communist Party. There were no standards of proof, no test of "reasonable doubt" such as in a courtroom, no rules of evidence, no opportunity to learn the origin of the charge or the identity of her accuser. Many of the people who were accused of disloyalty had joined front groups, in New York, or Chicago, or they had come from radical backgrounds. Not she. "In a sense it was my undoing; I could never repent, because I'd never done anything. I'd never been drawn to the Communist Party. So we felt good in that. No Fifth Amendment. We denied it."

There was no reason to feel good.

Her FBI file sheds considerable light on the origins of the charge —and on the procedures and premises that guided and governed these inquisitions.

"Your father kept saying, 'Prove it, show it, how do you know this?' And of course it always came back to some anonymous informant or another. I remember Al kept saying, 'You must have mistaken this because Mrs. Geller has been secretary of Local 203, that

173

must be what you mean when you say "secretary-treasurer of the underground." ' "

"This is very troubling," my father said to the board; and they agreed. "Can't we get that person here? That's just an infamous lie, and Mrs. Geller is willing to risk her neck on the perjury laws. There are prosecutions under the Loyalty Order. Can't we get that party in here? That's just an infamous lie."

"I wish we could, but we can't," responded a board member.

Still, the board decided Emily Geller was a threat to the national security of the United States and disloyal; she was dismissed from government service.

Chapter 23

That night, after he had spent an eight-hour day immersed in the files, I took my father to the Mets game. From Grand Central we rode the subway to Shea. He kept score, as he always does ("It's part of the game"), his own system, not so elaborate as to keep his eye off the game, but detailed enough to know what happened in previous innings. I tucked my program under the seat, though I know how to keep perfect score; I get hopelessly mired in the minutiae of the exercise, miss the big picture. The Mets won, 6–4 over Cincinnati, a great ninth inning, box seats on the third-base line. Baseball was always our game. To go to Griffith Stadium which was down the hill from the laundromat, we rode the trolley. Once, sitting in the upper-deck grandstand, we saw DiMaggio hit three homers at a Sunday doubleheader; I was a Yankee fan, he always rooted for the Senators. On our way into the park old Clark Griffith would be standing on the ramp by the ticket windows, always dressed in a white linen suit against the heat, and he'd tip his straw hat to those of us he knew as regular customers.

"In all these files I might have lost ten cases," my father said over breakfast the next morning. The FBI had noted the same fact repeatedly: "Bernstein has handled a considerable number of cases before government loyalty boards, and has been quite successful at it."

By then he had looked at perhaps a hundred cases. "In no case was a perjury charge ever filed," he repeated. "You had case after case with flat denials of membership in the Party." He had filled a legal pad with notes. "Which gets back to the real issue: Communism isn't the issue. That shows they were really trying to decimate the leadership of the union."

He spent the next couple of hours reading from the files of the Senate Internal Security Subcommittee, until we took a break to watch the opening of the Iran-Contra hearings. General Secord was testifying. Arthur Liman, chief counsel for the Senate in those hearings, was questioning him. "Boy, this is going to be rough," my father said, not without some admiration for Liman's style. He lay across my bed, a copy of his own testimony on his lap, from *Hearings into Subversive Control of the United Public Workers of America, Washington, D.C., 1951.*

"Haven't I got a right to counsel?" my father had asked Eastland.

The Senator had just sworn him: "Will you hold up your hand please. Do you solemnly swear the testimony you are about to give before the subcommittee of the Committee on the Judiciary of the Senate of the United States is the truth, the whole truth, and nothing but the truth, so help you God?"

"I do," said my father.

He had no way of knowing what the committee had prepared for him, but it is all there in the files, locked away for years in the Federal Records Center, a flat red-brick mausoleum off the Suitland Parkway, in Maryland.

"This is an executive session," Eastland told him.

My father again requested—formally, for the record—that he be permitted to have counsel.

176

"The request is denied."

"I wish to consult with counsel."

"You do not have that right. This is an investigation by the Senate, which is investigating treason and a bunch of traitors, and we have the right to ask you whatever questions we want."

He does not remember what Eastland's face looked like that day. I always picture the Senator with a cigar, for that is usually how I saw him, in his office or sometimes on the Senate subway, a cigar chomped down and spittle dripping from his mouth. On the day he left Washington for good, I ran into him at National Airport. He was wearing a Panama hat, getting on the plane I had just come off. He spotted me and came over to say goodbye. There had been occasions when he was a surprisingly helpful source of information. He put his arm around me, and I could see he was near tears.

"I thought the most miserable felon had a right to counsel," my father said.

"You are not on trial," the Senator said and began the series of questions prepared by the committee's counsel.

———

Mr. Raymond Mosley
Assistant Director
Washington National Records Center
Washington D.C. 20409

February 6, 1979

DEAR MR. MOSLEY:

Mr. Carl Bernstein has requested access to File 73-A-1375, Box 11, a folder containing papers of the Senate Internal Security Subcommittee located at the Federal Records Center in Suitland, Maryland. The Senate Historian has reviewed this file, as well as File 46-74-005, Box 17, and recommended that access be granted to Mr. Bernstein for both files. Accordingly, the access requested

177

by Mr. Bernstein is granted to review the materials contained in both File 73-A-1375, Box 11, and File 46-74-005, Box 17.

Sincerely, EDWARD M. KENNEDY
Chairman Senate Committee on the Judiciary

———

The historian's review noted that Box 17 was marked "Alfred David Bernstein" and contained "a dozen pages of background material, and suggested questions, with 'correct' answers, prepared for the 1951 hearings.

"The passage of more than a quarter of a century has effectively removed the sensitivity of both files," the historian added—though it had done nothing to remove *my* sensitivity, the more so after I had read the files. "Additionally," the historian said, "Bernstein would appear to have the right to information gathered on his parents."

The basic document relating to my father, and to the hearings into the union, is a memorandum dated July 10, 1951, to the committee's counsel from an investigator on the staff, suggesting that public testimony be taken. "There is no question we could have a good hearing on it. There is some work that should be done, however, on the project, before it is suitable for presentation." It described the problems and the objectives:

> In the first place, the two witnesses which CIO had to testify as to the Communist infiltration of the UPWA are wholly unreliable and Tom Harris of CIO tells me that CIO is sorry they called these two men. . . . This means we have to start practically from scratch in getting live witnesses who can testify as to Communist Party membership on the part of UPWA officials.

The next paragraph identified the targets:

> The three major figures in UPWA are Abraham Flaxer, Alfred David Bernstein, who lives in Washington, and Ewart Guinier. . . . We have a wealth of information on all three of these individ-

178

uals from the FBI and it will serve very nicely as a basis for interrogation.

The FBI was misinformed about my father's membership in the Party. His accuser was Jim Gorham, with whom he had worked on Capitol Hill during the railroad investigation in the late thirties. The FBI files state that Gorham informed the Bureau that my father had been in the Party when they were working together with Max Lowenthal; next to this my father has penciled, "Wrong." He wasn't a Party member then, was not until he had been on the Coast for a time, not until 1942. After he returned to Washington from the Army, he and my mother drifted from the Party; neither had gone to Party meetings after 1947. And by 1951 the Bureau was having trouble finding anyone who actually knew whether he had ever been in the Party.

> Bernstein was director of negotiations for UPWA and as such represented numerous government employees who were also members of UPWA and who were before loyalty boards [the memorandum continued]. . . . On February 20, 1949 Bernstein attended a National Lawyers Guild convention in Detroit. He said at the time that it was a good opportunity to discuss loyalty cases and techniques with other liberal lawyers.
>
> I asked Nichols if he had a witness who could put Bernstein in the party in the event he tells us he is not a member and Nichols said he would cross that bridge when he came to it and indicated that he could probably furnish such a witness.

Nichols was Louis B. Nichols—Bud Nichols—the assistant director of the FBI for internal-security matters and, later, the Bureau's liaison to Richard Nixon's White House.

"I entered as a private and came out as a buck sergeant," my father said on the witness stand in 1951. "I served overseas for a considerable portion of that time in the jungles of the Pacific."

"What battles were you in?" the Senator asked.

"I was in no battles. I was attached to the Air Force. I was under quite a few raids where I was. I saw enough action to satisfy me. When I returned I entered the employ of the United Public Workers of America and I guess that was about November 1945."

"Who owns this launderette in Washington?"

"I own it myself."

"Did anyone finance the laundry for you?"

Apparently the committee was prepared to expose a conspiracy to wash socks in Washington.

My father had opened the laundry that spring of 1951 with the small amount of money his father had left him. By then there was really no union left to work for; it had been expelled from the CIO (with a lot of help from the FBI and the two aforementioned unreliable witnesses) on February 16, 1950, along with 25 percent of the total membership of the CIO, for alleged Communist influence. UPW's locals were going under or reaffiliating with other AFL unions; thousands of its members had been through loyalty-board proceedings.

"In 1947 you testified before the House Committee on Education and Labor, is that correct?" counsel resumed. "That was a special subcommittee to investigate a GSI strike, wasn't it? . . . I would like to read you some testimony, Mr. Bernstein, of yours before the House Committee . . . Mr. Hoffman posing the question."

MR. HOFFMAN: You are not interested in whether the American communist organization or those who belong to it get their orders from their parent organization in Russia.
MR. BERNSTEIN: I am not interested in the communist organization. I am interested in earning a living for my family and working at my job. That is a big problem these days.
MR. HOFFMAN: You think the Loyalty Board order is unfair, do you?
MR. BERNSTEIN: I think it is disgraceful as a piece of business.

180

"Did you say that?" Senator Eastland's counsel asked now.

"Yes, sir."

"How did you get your job with the OPA?" Senator Eastland resumed.

"The Fifth Amendment."

"Was it some Communist who took you into the OPA?"

"The Fifth Amendment."

"Did you commit some crime in getting into the OPA?"

"The Fifth Amendment."

"Who recommended you for the position with the OPA?"

"The Fifth Amendment, sir."

"Whom did you give as character references when you got this job with the OPA?"

"Fifth Amendment."

To answer any of the questions would have opened a line of inquiry requiring my father to talk about membership in the Communist Party, and about other people. One of the names the committee wanted to dwell on, according to the staff's preparatory notes, was Max Lowenthal; the FBI had sent over a dossier on my father which noted that Lowenthal had been responsible for hiring him when he first came to Washington; Lowenthal, who was perhaps Harry Truman's best friend before Truman became President, was described in the dossier as a known Communist—a preposterous notion, but perhaps best explained by the fact that in 1950 he had written the first major book critical of the FBI under J. Edgar Hoover.

"Did you break with the Communist Party at the time you disassociated yourself from the United Public Workers of America?" my father was asked.

"I decline to answer that question on the ground of the Fifth Amendment."

"Were you a member of the Communist Party prior to the enactment of the Smith Act in 1940?"

The Smith Act had, in effect, outlawed membership in the Communist Party; made it a crime to belong to any organization "advocating the violent overthrow" of the U.S. government. More than one hundred members of the Party were convicted under the act, before the Supreme Court threw out their convictions in 1957.

"The same answer," my father said.

By then he had taken the Fifth Amendment twenty-four times.

"Mr. Chairman, I respectfully suggest the witness be ordered and directed to answer that question."

"Yes; I order and direct you to answer that question."

"I am sorry, sir."

"Who is Louise Bransten?" asked counsel.

"I decline to answer that question on the ground of the Fifth Amendment."

"Do you know Louise Bransten?"

"I know Louise Bransten."

"When did you last see her?"

"I decline to answer that question on the ground—"

"Louise Bransten is a Soviet intelligence agent living in New York, is she not?"

"The same answer to that question."

"Did you visit with Louise Bransten in 1944 when you were in the Army?"

"The same answer."

"When did you last see her?"

"The same answer."

"Let the record show I am ordering him to answer each and every one of those questions," Senator Eastland interjected.

Counsel resumed. "How do you know there is an individual known as Louise Bransten?"

"The same answer."

"You testified that you know there is an individual by the name of Louise Bransten."

"Yes, sir."

"You have opened up that area of inquiry. I am now asking you when you first saw her."

"The same answer."

"Mr. Chairman, I respectfully suggest if the record doesn't so show that he be ordered and directed to answer these questions."

"The record shows he is ordered and directed to answer each and every one of those questions," said Eastland.

"He has admitted in the record that he knows Louise Bransten," counsel continued. "Did you know Louise Bransten while you were wearing the uniform of this country?"

"The same answer."

"How long have you known Louise Bransten?"

"The same answer."

Somewhere subconsciously there was always the fear that I would stumble onto something, fall upon some parental Pumpkin Paper that would forever close me off to my parents. And that fear too, the dread of what I might find, contributed to the decision to abandon the project. I recall the fear as I waited in the reading room of the Library of Congress for the green-covered volumes of governmental inquiry containing my father's name; and that was the fear each time I came upon his testimony before Eastland, and read the exchanges about Louise Bransten.

> QUESTION: When you were a sergeant in the Air Corps, wearing the uniform of this country, you visited Louise Bransten on the West Coast, didn't you? Specifically on March 13, 1944. [That is Number 25 on the list of suggested questions prepared for my father's testimony by the committee staff.]
> ANSWER: Bureau files reflect that is true.

"On 3/13/44 Bernstein, then a Master Sergeant in the Air Corps, was present at the home of Louise Bransten. Bransten was a confident [sic] of numerous Soviet Intelligence agents including Gregori Kheifits who was the West Coast director of Soviet intelligence in the United States for several years."

That is the extent of information in the Bureau's files.

26. What did you and Louise Bransten talk about?
27. Was this a regular Communist Party meeting or was this a special assignment?

In fact it was a social event—a party, as my father recalls.

"Have you ever had occasion to discuss with Communist Party officials the availability of information to be procured from the United States Government agencies by members of the United Public Workers?" my father was asked on the witness stand.

"No," he answered.

"Do you know of any discussions between the Communist Party hierarchy and the officials of the United Public Workers of America?"

"No."

There was nothing ambivalent.

The final questioning was about his income. He testified that he had been paid $4,600 a year by the union.

"Did you have any other sources of income besides your salary with the union?" Eastland asked.

"I would like to discuss that with my lawyer."

"Will you answer the question?"

"I would like to discuss it with my lawyer. I don't know that that is a proper question."

"Do you decline to answer the question?"

"I would appreciate discussing it with my lawyer."

"No; we are not going to permit that. Will you answer the question."

"I don't know what that could have to do with internal security," my father said.

"Maybe you do not," replied the Senator.

"Let me answer this way: The other sources of my income that I have have nothing to do with internal security."

184

"Will you answer the question about your other sources of income?"

"I will be glad to answer the question if my lawyer thought it was a proper one. I really don't know if it is a proper one, Mr. Chairman."

"I want you to answer the question. It is not up to your lawyer to determine whether a question in this hearing is proper."

"I think I am entitled to the advice of counsel on that question."

"You are not going to get it. You decline to answer at your peril."

"I will decline to answer."

"How does it make you feel?" I asked him.

I was lying next to him on the bed. On television, Chairman Lee H. Hamilton was speaking to General Secord.

"It's a long time ago, Carl. I'm not exercised, if that's what you mean, I've come to terms, you know, the years." My father thought a moment. "When I looked at those flyers, that was really what we were about. We were the only effective organization in the government at the time. We were the only real union."

The flyers, mimeographed union bulletins, had been collected by the FBI and sent to Suitland. They seemed almost touching in their naiveté, full of clarion calls to join the union and illustrated with stick figures carrying picket signs—pages lovingly prepared and, it occurred to me, not dissimilar in form to those I used to type and stencil when I was editor of the *Lincoln Torch*.

"United Public Workers scored an historic victory on Friday, Jan. 12, 1950 when 17 Negro veterans of World War II began their training as apprentices in the plate printing craft at the Bureau of Engraving," one page began. "Until that day the plate printing craft had been exclusively lily white at the Bureau. The Negro vets will receive journeyman's pay of $25 per day."

There were leaflets: "Win a wage increase. Join the Union." Appeals for cost-of-living allowances: "Coffee, 25 to 85 cents a pound from 1941 to 1950; porkchops, 27 cents to 80 cents: Join the

185

union"; a demand for improvement of lighting conditions in one of the federal buildings where proofreaders and typesetters worked.

> Vending machines? Swell Recreation Club? Very good. But wonderful as these innovations are, they do not alleviate the grievances and discomforts that employees of the Immigration and Naturalization Service Suffer—What about pressure due to work sheets? What about constant watchfulness on the part of supervisors? What about cement floors? Do you really want to have your working conditions improved: then do as Government workers Everywhere are Doing. Join the United Public Workers of America, CIO BECAUSE UPW/CIO fights for better salaries; improved working conditions; elimination of efficiency ratings to remove favoritism and discrimination; liberalized retirement laws; no reduction in force; unemployment insurance, severance pay. COME TO OUR SPRING PARTY, FRIDAY MAY 6TH, UNION HALL. . . .

"That was what we were all about," my father said. He glanced at General Secord and looked away.

"They never asked about what I did in the union. They never asked me what my function was. They weren't interested. They weren't interested in anything, apparently, except what my political policies might be. The one trend that runs through all the testimony in that volume is, What do you know about other people?—as opposed to what people were doing at that time, why they were active, what the union's function was, what it had achieved."

I remembered the metal dash of the old Plymouth, and again I wanted to hold him near, hug him, but all I would allow myself was a playful tousle of the hair straining over his forehead as he lay next to me.

"What were the extra sources of income?" I asked my father.

"Poker," he said.

186

Chapter 24

"This is amazing, but it's the truth," my father said the next morning. He was holding a memo written on old *Washington Post* six-ply, the summary of an interview with Clark Clifford, the eminence of Democratic Party politics.

"*It was a political problem.* Truman was going to run in '48, and that was it."

For a minute my father continued to stare at the memo.

"Can you quote him?"

I nodded.

"He says it a few times," I noted. "He won't deny it."

"You could write a book, Carl. It's the smoking gun of the whole Loyalty Order. That's an incredible piece of information."

"I couldn't believe it when he said it," I responded finally; indeed, when I heard it, I'd sat in a state of perfect reportorial impassion—expressionless, motionless, save for the scratchings of an unsteady hand in a notebook.

"That word 'manufacture'—the way he uses it," my father said. "That explains all the stuff we've been talking about, all that crap they had to go to: the Bookshop Association, membership in the American Labor Party, the list of subversive organizations—because there was nothing there, there was no real political activity of any sort in the Communist Party, no threat." He paused. "It was really a war against liberals.

"This business about Hoover feeding him information on his enemies . . ." He read through the whole memo again. "You better finish that book before he dies." He laughed. "He's as old as me."

As if to himself, "They never showed anybody *doing anything* who was alleged to be a Communist. They never showed him in a conspiratorial meeting, they never showed him doing something subversive. It's all manufactured. I said that time and time again. When they say someone's a Communist they never show him anywhere, they never show him doing anything."

He wondered whether Charlie Murphy was still alive. I said yes; I'd gone to the other surviving members of Truman's inner circle and confirmed the information. First I'd gone to Bob Donovan, who covered the Truman White House for the *New York Herald Tribune* and, in the 1970s, had written an authoritative account of the Truman years, a two-volume history. Only six pages are devoted to the Loyalty Order, in *Conflict and Crisis*, the first volume—but they are on target: "The Order," he wrote, "certainly produced some deplorable results for a Constitutional democracy."

"It's an amazing interview," my father repeated now.

I showed him the text of another interview—with Joseph Rauh, the noted civil-liberties lawyer. In it, Joe related how he and a group of insiders were sitting around the Oval Office with Truman after he had decided finally not to seek reelection, in 1951.

"Well, how'd I do, boys, how'd you grade me?" HST apparently asked them. And according to Joe, they all gave him high marks, except on the Loyalty Order, which Joe brought up. He claims he told Truman that it was the worst thing he had done, that it had helped poison the atmosphere. Joe said Truman grimaced and said, "Yes, it was terrible."

My father, however, seemed utterly uninterested in Truman's

188

purported response; instead he focused on Joe Rauh's comment to me that the Loyalty Order was, in his view, "excessive," that it had gone too far, especially in its failure to allow accused to confront accuser.

"Even Joe got scared," my father said. "If a guy had a case and he'd seen me first, Joe would warn him about me—that I was to the left. Joe, he wasn't the nicest guy involved. Let me put it a little differently, I want to be accurate: He refused to take cases."

Joe Rauh is probably the most revered elder of Washington's liberal establishment, a founding member of Americans for Democratic Action, holder of the Medal of Liberty of the American Civil Liberties Union. He has been a friend for years, someone I've always admired. I argued. He took some of the cases, I said.

"Not many. Not if somebody had a left-wing background and wanted to take his case before a loyalty board. The same with Arnold and Porter."

I have always had trouble with this contention of my father's, the idea that liberals, in their faintheartedness, are more to blame than the other side.

My father read over the first memorandum again, from an afternoon visit to Clark Clifford, years before.

"That 'manufactured' bit, that is amazing," he said again. "What year is that?"

I'd gone to see Clifford in December 1978.

"Oh, that's a hell of a document, Carl."

"Given everything you've said, how the Loyalty Order really started everything—" I started to ask a question.

"It's the heart of it," my father said. "Right here."

"My own notion was that there were merely some incidents," Clifford had told me. "My own feeling was there was not a serious loyalty problem. I felt the whole thing was being manufactured. We never had a serious discussion about a real loyalty problem."

He had met with the President every day, as his counsel. There had been a daily staff meeting at which the progress of the order was periodically discussed.

"I have the sensation that the President didn't attach fundamental importance to the so-called Communist scare. He thought it was a lot of baloney. But political pressures were such that he had to recognize it.

"We used to comment on the fact that as far as J. Edgar and the Congress were concerned there was a problem. The President had no regard for Hoover; he didn't like the way he went about his business.

"There was no substantive problem," he said, flatly. "It was a political problem. We did not believe there was a real problem. A problem was being manufactured. There was a certain element of hysteria. I don't believe any of us ever felt really threatened, Carl. I don't believe anything there constituted a genuine threat."

Throughout the interview I was struck by Clifford's imposing physical presence: tall, handsome, tanned, tailoring perfect, his bearing inseparable from the signs around him of a life in service to the country, to Presidents in particular, from Roosevelt to Carter— not the usual tokens of Washingtoniana and Oval Office photographs, but what seemed like an acreage of wall space and desk top attesting tangibly to his presence at the great events of our times.

On his desk—itself a study in order, a huge old partner's desk covered in leather—were some twenty piles of neatly stacked papers, note-sized, sorted and ready for filing, it seemed, each held down by a paperweight award or medal or gilded testament: the National Service Medal, a minted likeness of JFK, Truman's in bronze, HST's inaugural medal from '48.

"Later, the President—Truman—commented on McCarthy. I remember how outraged he was at the sheer reprehensibility of McCarthy. He talked about what a dangerous period that was for the country. McCarthy had taken a minor situation and used it for an enormous campaign of vilification and rousing people. In the afteryears he spoke of the danger when men of this kind appear on

190

the scene and whip people up and lead them away from the basic concept of our form of government."

For some reason, I was focusing on his clothes: brown wing-tip shoes, brown suit, striped shirt, brown spotted tie, a confectionery of chocolate and hazelnut.

At that point Clifford excused himself to take a call in an anteroom, from the President—Carter. On his desk, encased in a leather wallet embossed with the Great Seal, was his passport; he had returned the previous night from Algeria, where he had represented the United States at the funeral of the Algerian president.

Smiling, he strode back into the room after five minutes. He had just recommended to the President that Muhammad Ali be used in special goodwill ambassadorial roles to Third World countries. Ali had accompanied him back from Algiers; Clifford had been amazed at how people responded to him. "I always thought he was a big-mouth," he said. At Shannon Airport, he said, a hundred clerks had surrounded Ali in a frenzy. "We had a long talk; he recognizes that this country has been awfully good to him, and that he owes a debt to this country and he wants to repay it."

He eased back into the subject. "Why didn't he fire J. Edgar? He didn't trust him, he didn't like the way he operated. He could see enough of Hoover's operation to know it wasn't consistent with his own feelings of justice and fairness. . . . But J. Edgar was feeding information to Truman on his adversaries."

He described the situation leading to Truman's issuance of Executive Order 9835. "He was under enormous political pressures, and he was pushed into answering them. The issue was built to the point where he couldn't ignore it.

"We never had a serious discussion about a real loyalty problem," he repeated. "The whole attitude in the White House was what you might call 'liberal.' " He paused. "It was a response to the temper of the times."

He picked up one of the medals on his desk, gold, gleaming, gripping its rounded edges as if it were a discus.

"We were the only nation that had the bomb, we wanted to be sure that we were the only nation that had it. What was the couple that later were executed, I guess, for their efforts?"

"The Rosenbergs," I said.

"I have to admit it's a hazy vague part of the whole period."

But he spoke precisely about the promulgation of the Loyalty Order and the circumstances surrounding it. Tom Clark, the Attorney General, Ramsey's father, was in charge of the drafting; most of the input came from Hoover.

"The Un-American Activities Committee. . . . They were giving us trouble. The political implications of it were such that he could not do anything but issue it. He had to face up to it, and take some action with reference to it. There was the whole red-herring question: They beat him with it to a bloody stump. He had to recognize the political realities of life. He'd gotten a terrible clobbering in 1946 in the congressional elections. And for the next two years.

"We gave a good deal of thought to how to respond. We had a presidential campaign ahead of us and here was a great issue, a very damaging issue, so he set up this whole kind of machinery. How it functioned is an unknown chapter to me." He gestured with the discus. "Later on some men who were destroyed were reconstructed."

I asked him who came to mind.

He was silent.

Truman issued the order on March 21, 1947.

"The Loyalty Order was the Truman Administration's answer to the times," my father said.

In the spring of 1946, Winston Churchill had delivered his Iron Curtain speech in Fulton, Missouri. In June the Republican National Committee announced the theme of its fall election campaign: Communism or Republicanism. A good part of the hierarchy of the American Catholic Church joined the crusade. The voice of American business, the U.S. Chamber of Commerce, went into

192

battle, charging that Reds and fellow travelers had penetrated the federal service, especially the State Department and the government labor unions, i.e., the United Public Workers.

In Canada, twenty-two people, many of them employees of the Canadian government, were arrested that year by the Mounties on espionage charges. Soon afterward, J. Edgar Hoover sent Truman a secret report containing the revelations of Elizabeth Bentley, "the blond spy queen," as the newspapers called her later, when Hoover sent her before the House Committee on Un-American Activities to tell her story in public, three months before the presidential election. Truman had feared what Hoover and the Congress might do with inflammatory charges about spies in an election year, and in November 1946 he had appointed a Presidential Commission on Government Employee Loyalty. Its recommendations formed the basis of the Loyalty Order.

In the same week that he issued Executive Order 9835, Truman asked Congress to aid the Greek anti-Communist forces: the Truman Doctrine was being formulated; it would be difficult to seek aid against Communism abroad without doing something about the "Communist menace" at home.

I read aloud to my father Mark Geller's comment that the order was intended to wipe out the progressive forces.

"I like Clifford's analysis a little better," my father said. "I think it turned into something like Mark Geller described. I think it was a political motivation at the start."

To save their own asses?

"That's what Clifford is saying. If he had given some leadership, if the President had given some leadership, instead of coming up with this dreadful order, and said, 'Look, let's not panic about this' . . ."

It is his contention that the history of this country would have been different had Truman resisted.

"You don't think Truman intended it as what Mark says, as an onslaught against progressive people?"

"I don't think so. I think it developed that way. I think it got out of control. And he did nothing to stop the onslaught. He was acting like I'd expect him to act."

This is an old theme—leadership. Gary Hart had quit the race for the presidency that week—for the first time; at breakfast we were discussing the remaining field. A real leader, my father said, would deal with the question of housing in America first, solve the country's economic problems by rebuilding it, change the agenda, not be bound by reacting to what was already on the national plate. I think it was my father who first put the idea into my head that Ronald Reagan, however reactionary, might be a real leader—someone who fights for what he believes in, who pursues a different path.

In 1953, I. F. Stone wrote a book called *The Truman Era*, based largely on his newspaper columns of the time; Izzy's book is about how Truman failed as a leader, about what a small man he was—"a man without faith in himself, surrounded by men without real faith in American society." Truman did not believe in the Loyalty Order. But he initiated it.

"All I have to do is finish writing," I said.

"You've got all the research done? How are you going to handle notes, footnotes and things? Are you going to do it?"

"It's not that kind of book," I said. "It's a very personal book. It's not a history book at all." At which my father started pacing around a bit.

My father spent the rest of the morning studying cases. The key feature of the Loyalty Order was the creation by the Attorney General of a list of subversive organizations, membership in which (or association with, or even proximity to) was used by the loyalty boards to pass on an individual's loyalty to the country—and thus an individual's fitness to serve in the government.

"It allowed them to go into relationships, marriages, guilt by association, religious beliefs," my father was saying. "By the creation of the list it gave the impression that the government could do damn near anything."

"Did you ever notice that Mr. Beitscher wore a button of the Lincoln Brigade in his coat lapel?" Emily Geller was asked at her loyalty hearing.

> The departmental loyalty boards and the Loyalty Review Board were not judicial but administrative bodies [writes Robert Donovan in Volume I of his history of the Truman presidency], and for the first time administrative officials and agencies were authorized to inquire into and pass judgment on personal beliefs, associations and opinions of a private citizen employed or seeking employment in the government. . . . [T]he individual became the accused with no presumption of innocence to protect him. Persons were adjudged untrustworthy not because of overt wrongful acts but because of their ideas, because of motives attributed to them, or because of suspicion as to their future conduct. Established in American jurisprudence thereby was a doctrine of imputing guilt because of association. No provision was made for judicial review. . . .

Or for the cross-examination of witnesses, or the disclosure of evidence upon which the government relied, or the presentation of the government's case through the sworn testimony of witnesses in open hearing. "On the contrary," it was noted in *The Yale Law Review*, "the government's case against the employee will consist largely or wholly of the FBI report." No rules of evidence were required in this courtroom, no provisions made for any public hearing on which organizations the Attorney General designated "subversive," no single standard of proof of disloyalty was established from one government department to the next. The term "disloyalty" was never defined.

As John Lord O'Brian, senior attorney at Covington and Burling, former assistant to the Attorney General in the administration of Herbert Hoover, wrote, at the time, "it established in effect something like a new system of preventative law applicable to the field of ideas and essentially different from traditional American procedures."

Truman asked for a budget of $25 million for the first year to administer his Loyalty Order; Congress reduced the figure to $11 million for the first year and gave him $6,606,000 for the second. That compared to an annual budget of $2,991,000 for the National Labor Relations Board, with its staff of 1,033 employees; a budget of $5,560,000 for the Federal Communications Commission, with a staff of 1,422; and $2,519,120 for the Federal Trade Commission, with 582 employees.

"The size of the program," Donovan notes, "made it an administrative monstrosity."

Within weeks of its issuance, all employees subject to the order had been fingerprinted and instructed to answer questionnaires calling for various background data, including the names of organizations to which they belonged. By mid-September 1948, they had all undergone FBI checks: the bureau had found no derogatory information concerning 2,110,521 employees and had instituted full investigations of the remaining 6,344. Of these, 619 resigned during the course of their investigation, 44 were found to be no longer in government employment, and 923 investigations had not been completed. The remaining 4,758 cases were referred by the FBI to loyalty boards.

The records of those times, buttressed by the files that lay in our basement for so many years, reveal the whole engine of government hurtling down the track toward this group of people, few of them in sensitive positions in government, as far as I can determine. For this really was a witch-hunt. There were already an abundance of espionage laws on the books, and additional provisions and procedures whereby any government employee in a sensitive position could be dismissed for legitimate security reasons—in the Defense Department, the State Department, the CIA, the Atomic Energy Commission.

The Congress, emboldened by Truman's Loyalty Order, authorized new procedures in October 1947 under which employees of the sensitive agencies could henceforth be summarily dismissed for disloyalty. Among the new criteria for dismissal were "written evi-

196

dence or oral expressions by speeches or otherwise, of political, economic or social views."

An atmosphere of secrecy and fear in the government was one effect of Executive Order 9835, the requirement of political orthodoxy another. For the next two generations much of our politics was premised on the assumption of danger to our very system from certain people—people like my parents and their friends.

"Do you read a good many books?" "What magazines do you read?" "What newspapers do you buy or subscribe to?" "Do you think that Russian Communism is likely to succeed?" "How do you explain the fact that you have an album of Paul Robeson records in your home?" "Do you ever entertain Negroes in your home?" "Is it not true that you lived next door to and therefore were closely associated with a member of the IWW?" "Have you ever discussed the subject of the dance in Russia?" "Did you ever write a letter to the Red Cross about the segregation of blood?"

These were among the questions asked before loyalty boards.

Chapter 25

"Emily Geller's case was one of the few where I actually brought witnesses," my father was saying. Fourteen witnesses attested to her loyalty and ability. Affidavits were filed from every supervisor and boss she ever had. She spent two years fighting. Not a single derogatory witness or piece of documentary evidence against her was introduced in the proceedings; only the unsubstantiated allegations from the FBI's files, and the vague charges of the interrogatory. She testified under oath, aware of the risk of perjury. "We had convinced them of enough that they shouldn't have believed this stuff. It is shocking what they did."

Her denial of membership in the Party, and of participation in activities of the Party, was unequivocal. "I am not now and I have never been a member of the Communist Party or similar organization," she said.

Still, the burden of proof was on her.

MR. EXAMINER: Would you know any reason why certain individuals whose integrity has never been questioned and who over a long period of time have been reliable would state that you were or are a member of the Communist Party?

MRS. GELLER: The only reason I can think of is it could have been out of sheer malice—

MR. BERNSTEIN: You said reliable people stated that she was a member of the Communist Party. These people, may we know who they are?

"That information is not given out," the chairman of the loyalty board responded.

In fact, the chairman did not know. J. Edgar Hoover had told the President's Temporary Commission on Loyalty that information on Communists and the Party would dry up if the FBI were forced to disclose such evidence—even *in camera* to a loyalty board. Hoover had threatened to withdraw publicly from participation in the President's Loyalty Program rather than agree to disclose the evidence, and Truman had consented.

The examiner resumed: "How would you explain, Mrs. Geller, that members of the Communist Party consider you a member of the Communist Party?"

"As far as I know, I don't know any members of the Communist Party. So I don't know how they consider me as such."

"Information indicates that you have been instrumental in contacting and placing new Communist Party members in the unit of the Government Group," he asserted.

"Would you state that over, please?"

"In 1945 a member of the Communist Party stated you had selected him or her to go into the Government underground group of the Communist Party."

"As far as I am concerned, that charge is absolutely ridiculous," she said to the loyalty board. It would be another thirty years before Emily could comprehend exactly what had happened.

The examiner was not called a prosecutor. "Do the members of the

Board have any questions in regard to Mrs. Geller's membership in the Communist Party?" he asked. He did not use the word "alleged."

There were no questions.

At the beginning of the hearing, the chairman of the loyalty board was forthright about the nature of the proceedings: "This isn't strictly a legal proceeding," he told Emily. "We do not follow any such rules."

And the tortured logic was stated at the outset. "This is an administrative hearing by your employer, the Government, for the benefit of yourself as a prospective employee of the Government, and we want you to feel perfectly at ease," he told Emily.

Among other things, she was accused of "having replaced one Olivia Israeli Abelson as Secretary of the Government underground group shortly after April, 1946, when she ceased to function in the position due to pregnancy."

"Absolutely untrue. Absolutely untrue. It is a mere charge," Emily protested.

"Do you know anyone by the name of Annie Stein or Arthur Stein?" she was asked. The question immediately preceded the one about the Abraham Lincoln Brigade lapel pin.

Emily said she knew Arthur Stein as an officer of the union. "And Annie Stein I know slightly. . . . I will explain to you how I know her. She was a worker for the Domestic Workers Union and I remember calling the union to find out if they could get me a day worker and then I didn't really see her until about last year."

Though the literature of the period is filled with allusions to Communists taking over the labor movement, I have yet to encounter a reference to plots to organize Washington's maids. Still, there is something devilishly appealing about the idea. Basically, Annie organized black people and women; when I saw her last she was the principal organizer of the Ocean Hill–Brownsville movement for neighborhood control of schools in New York City.

200

"Annie Stein was an officer in the Washington Committee for Consumer Protection . . . a group, as I recall, of women who worked on consumer problems like price control. . . . That was about the time that President Truman was concerned with requests to reestablish OPA and the whole question of whether or not there should be controls," Emily testified; she had helped to book speakers. "They spoke at schools, all over, and at PTA meetings, that is how I know Mrs. Stein."

("Truman should have welcomed us instead of coming after us," my father noted. "We were doing things in the community that were on his agenda: consumer issues, fighting discrimination, women's rights, extending the New Deal. The Progressive Party in 1948 got over a million votes, and that's who we *really* are. We are part of that progressive coalition. Among other things we were against the Loyalty Order and the Cold War.")

"Do you know a Betty Hayes?" This question was from the chairman of the loyalty board.

One of the more intriguing entries in my parents' FBI files is about Betty and Bill Hayes. It states that the Bureau knew they were not members of the Communist Party, but that they should be considered dangerous because they knew or associated with members of the Party and supported causes known to be favored by the Party. Accordingly, the Bureau continued to keep them under surveillance through the 1960s.

"Betty Hayes was chairman of the Labor Canteen that the union ran during the war, and I was a hostess at the Labor Canteen and that is how I know Mrs. Hayes," Emily told the loyalty board. "She was in charge of the hostesses. She was a senior hostess because most of us were much younger."

"Is it or is it not true that you attended a picnic of the Washington Bookshop Association sometime in July of 1946?" the examiner asked.

"I don't know. I really don't know. I am just trying to think of whether I was in Washington in July 1946."

MR. EXAMINER: Did you ever attend any picnics in 1946, before or after that?

MRS. GELLER: I really don't know. I don't think so but I don't know. It is certainly nothing that stands out in my mind. It was never of any importance.

MR. EXAMINER: You mean you couldn't remember whether you attended any picnic about that time of year?

A word on the subject of picnics, Mr. Examiner: They were awful. They were endless. They happened every weekend, way the hell off in Anacostia, past Bolling Air Force Base—up the big hill to Congress Heights, and over to the mosquito-infested field at Wheeler Road and Mississippi Avenue. From the top of Nichols Avenue you could look down at the tiny fighters on the flight line at Bolling, and across the river, shimmering through the heat, the Capitol. Then the fighters would rise like gnats, silent until they were level with Nichols Avenue, and soon they would be directly overhead, at treetop level, and then everything shook.

Picnics for integration, picnics to freeze the price of pork, picnics to protest the Loyalty Order, picnics—and always there were huge mosquitoes.

"Well, we always have a lot of picnics," Emily Geller told the loyalty board. "We had picnics, personal picnics where you take your lunch and go to the park, just friends, and the union had a lot of picnics—that was one of our summer activities. There was a time that we had a picnic almost every Sunday, and so I just can't say."

"You say that you can't identify this particular one?"

"It doesn't mean anything. We still go to picnics when we are home in Washington, because it is so much cooler outside."

At such picnics (this child is prepared to testify), there was never a word about overthrowing the government. There were always picnics on July Fourth, and once my mother twisted her ankle in a potato-sack race and had to go to the hospital and I had to wait outside with my father and I cried. It is true there *were* songs about owning those banks of marble and sharing those vaults of silver, but

202

allegiance to a foreign power? Taking violent action against the government of the United States? Spying? Treason? Pete Seeger sang sometimes, and Cisco Houston. Listen to those songs. I remember speeches also, not the words exactly, but the feel, a lot of talk, no doubt, about making this country a better place, decent, more humane—the same stuff they always seemed to be saying.

The text of Emily's hearing reads as if translated from the Russian, its mind-set borrowed from the Moscow trials, or perhaps *1984* —very different from the HUAC proceedings, which are blatant, the purpose of the committee naked and apparent: to expose and shame.

These examiners and board members are not demagogues or charlatans. Rather they are earnest patriots and bureaucrats imbued with the seriousness and sanctity of their charge: to protect the state from disloyalty. And, as believers in the threat, and in their own rectitude and in the rectitude of all governmental machinery, they exude an air of reasonableness quite at odds with their words and actions.

"There are no charges against Mrs. Geller," the chairman said to my father. It was a rebuke. "The Board does not make charges. This Board receives information about people. It then makes inquiry of those people as to the facts. We are purely fact-finding. We do not make any charges at all against any Government employee."

> Specifically, and in support of the above, the Board has been informed that you have been closely associated with the following individuals, all of whom reportedly are past or present members of the Communist Party and/or its Front organizations.
>
> Donald Murray, Anne Rosen, Annie Stein, Arthur Stein, Shirley Taylor, (Mrs. William C.) Betty Hayes, Henry Beitscher, Sylvia Beitscher, Rose Cummins, Edith Cummins, Mickey (Milton, Michael) Salkind, Nettie Eisman (Ned Kramer, Net Rosen, Ned Eisman), Olivia Israeli (Mrs. Abelson).

"Another matter I am a little vague on is that reference to Donald Murray." The chairman was addressing Emily. "I believe you said that he had something to do with some chorus."

"Yes. The United Federal Workers Chorus. We had a recreational program until 1941, 1942, I think. After that, because of the pressure of work, people just didn't have time for recreation. One of the activities that we had was a chorus and I was in that chorus. That chorus sang at the White House, I believe in 1942, and I knew him from that."

There is a lot about music in the transcript, which is fitting, because the music was always evocative of the reality:

MR. EXAMINER: Do you recall, Mrs. Geller, that at any of the union meetings that you might have attended that the Communist song, the Internationale, had been sung?

MRS. GELLER: I don't know the song. I never heard anything with that name sung. We always sang union songs and only union songs, folk songs.

Even at the shule we never sang "The Internationale."

"Do you know Henry Beitscher?"

(He was the one with the Lincoln Brigade pin in his lapel.)

She had known him as an active member of Local 203, Emily testified.

"Do you know him very well?"

"Well, I knew him very well in the sense that we had worked together in the union."

"Do you know anything about the Abraham Lincoln Brigade? Ever hear of it? You know anything about the general reputation—as being connected with the Communist organizations?"

"I have just heard about them. I don't know anything about them," Emily said.

"I am asking, did you ever hear that they were considered subversive?"

"I have heard that about them."

"Did you ever notice that Mr. Beitscher wore a button of the brigade in his coat lapel?"

"No I never did. I wouldn't have recognized it if I had seen it."

"You wouldn't have recognized it?"

"No. I have never seen one. I didn't know there was such a thing."

"You have never had any connection through him with the Lincoln Brigade?"

"No—"

A member of the loyalty board interrupted. "Have you any idea who might have been so unfriendly with you or have had malice against you that would have caused them to make such statements that might link you with the Communist Party or any Communist organization?"

"All I can do is reconstruct the picture as I get it from you gentlemen," she said. "Because many of these specific issues—questions, you know, have completely floored me.

"No, I just can't. I think it is, as I say—I can only go back to my original statement that there may be certain people who think that being an active union member is synonymous with being a member of the Communist Party, but other than that I can think of no way whereby anybody could say that about me.

"I contacted all my employers when this case came up and I have discussed it with them in great length. They stated that they have known me on the job and socially and have always considered me a loyal and patriotic American citizen and loyal government worker. . . .

"The only thing I could think that could be— I was Secretary of Local 203 of the United Federal Workers that later became the United Public Workers of America, and as Secretary of the organization I received mail and I sent out correspondence and conducted regular duties, and at the time I was employed—during part of that time I was employed by OPA and it was a well-known fact that I was Secretary of Local 203, it was a well-known fact and perhaps somebody could have misinterpreted that."

Indeed, that appears to have happened—and as well to Dorothy Bailey, who was president of Local 10 of the Federal Workers. In each instance, the vague and imprecise characterization by a hostile, anonymous accuser triggered the new machinery of this Loyalty Order.

The interrogatories would be spread over the dining-room table. My father would sit at the far end, where I'd sit at dinner, in front of the old buffet that had been in my Grandmother Bernstein's living room.

"I'd see what the interrogatory says; I'd go over them. I'd say, 'Let's go through them. Do we have an answer to each of the allegations?' " The strangers would be sitting adjacent to him, on the side of the table where my mother sat at dinner, usually a man and a woman together. "Some weren't even political people—mail carriers who had been to a meeting of something, charwomen who were in the union."

"If the accusation was technically right, say somebody was a member of the Bookshop Association, then what did you do?" I asked.

"Then you try to show why they are members of the organization. The Bookshop, the League against War and Fascism—that was the big one."

I was interested in knowing which organizations, aside from the Communist Party, had been the most difficult to defend membership in, to deal with allegations about. "I can't answer that. Because I'd treat them all the same. I'd treat them factually. For instance, 'Yes, I joined the League against War and Fascism, before World War II. Why? I'm Jewish. I was concerned about Hitler.' If I'm not Jewish: 'I was concerned about war with the Germans, about the buildup of the German and Italian armies, and I felt this was an organization that was doing something about it; there were very few of them doing anything about it before the U.S. entered the war.' Et cetera.

"With the Bookshop there were various reasons. One, you could buy books at a discount. Two, it had some cultural programs. They had lectures. If you really want to do the Bookshop, the big case we

206

won was Marie Siegrist, who was the last president of the Book-shop." Which is why I have a first-day-cover collection today. It was easy to picture her as the president of a bookshop, or a librarian, a plainly dressed, pretty woman with her hair tied back in a bun.

"Those loyalty hearings, you went in and really your only chance to win a case was to somehow justify the substance of the allegations on their [the board's] terms."

And here he explained something I'd had no comprehension of, even from reading the historical accounts about these proceedings:

"What I'm trying to say is that you could never go in there and say, 'Hey, sure I joined the Bookshop. I thought the Bookshop was a hell of an organization. I believed in their politics and I'm glad I belonged to it.' You had to hide what you believed in. That's the distinction, because under the Loyalty Order the atmosphere had become different and you couldn't keep your job and say you still believed in these things.

"So every case was handled in a defensive posture. You wanted to win the case and you couldn't say 'I did these things because I thought they were right and I still think they're right.' Because if you did that you'd be dead.

"Basically, you had to disavow your beliefs, you had no choice."

Today I understand all too well what my father was saying.

"And that kind of thing might have turned off people from going through it, and they resigned instead."

He rubbed his brow and thought a minute. "It's very interesting. Even if you read the names of the McCarthy stuff, his lists, they were almost all small people. They came out of the Loyalty Order, even the people attacked in the McCarthy Committee, that dentist. Small people. And the Loyalty Order made that respectable."

"Yes, well I joined the Washington Bookshop because of the dis-count privileges," Emily Geller testified. "I bought a lot of books. I have a very large family and we always exchanged books as presents, and so I could save considerable money on that. They had

207

paintings at a discount and I have always been interested in having paintings, and I joined for that reason, and also it was a cooperative and I have always felt that cooperatives were good organizations. I joined in pretty much the same way I joined Group Health. Which is a cooperative, because of the financial savings to the person who joins."

"Why did you pick the Washington Bookshop in preference to other bookshops around town?" the examiner pressed.

"I didn't know any others that gave discounts. I still don't know of any that gave discounts, and as I said, the fact that it was a cooperative meant an important thing to me."

Later, Bobby Bialek, who had gone to the shule with my mother when they were children, opened Discount Records and Books in the Dupont Circle Building, downstairs from where the graphic artists, some of them blacklisted, made their offices. When Emily had exhausted all her appeals, and the Bailey case had been lost, Emily went to work as the switchboard operator for the graphic artists at Presentations Incorporated, the cooperative they started.

"Why did you discontinue your membership in 1946, if you did?" the examiner asked.

"I just found myself going down there less and less. It was an inconvenient neighborhood, and I was working downtown—it just wasn't worth it; it was very much to me financial, and I suppose unconsciously I read and heard that it was considered to be a subversive organization—although I had never seen anything subversive about it. I had never been interested and never been too interested or active and I don't—I didn't see any point to continuing my membership, and I just let it lapse."

It was at that point that the examiner asked, "Is it true or is it not true that you attended a picnic of the Washington Bookshop Association sometime in July of 1946?" A picnic where, presumably, somebody from the FBI saw Emily talking to somebody wearing a lapel pin from the Abraham Lincoln Brigade.

208

The Washington Bookshop went out of business, killed by the Loyalty Order.

I have a manila envelope, addressed in the same hand as my first-day covers from Marie Siegrist, filled with material on the Bookshop, much of it unabashedly left-wing, relics of another time. There are also letters from Knopf, from Simon and Schuster, from other major publishing houses, attesting to the Bookshop's excellence and to the "American" cast of its inventory. There are copies of a mimeographed monthly newsletter which carried book reviews and bulletins ("The Washington Cooperative Bookshop, an interracial cultural organization, giving everyday evidence of the fundamental brotherhood of all people, annually honors and pays homage to the contributions of the Negro People to American democracy, on the occasion of Negro History Week"). On the back page of the Christmas issue, a dove of peace perches next to a naively stenciled Statue of Liberty.

In 1977, shortly after I had left the paper, I visited the Gellers in Los Angeles. Mark was working part time as an economist; he had sold storm doors for quite a while before that, until they moved West and times started to change; she is a social worker there.

"That television you got was a farewell present from the union," Emily remembered. "Mark and I did the collecting. We got two hundred fifty dollars. That's how we used to spend many Saturday nights. Your father was involved in the goddamn laundromat, and I guess we went to your house on Saturday nights because your father was so beat.

"I always tell the story to my clients," Emily continued, "when they have children and nobody is relating to each other: I tell them I had these friends who lived in chaos, in absolute chaos; but one thing I always remembered: that the world could be coming to an end in that house, and believe me, Carl, it very often felt that way, but at a certain time it would all stop and in this living room which was a *mess* your mother would bring out hors d'oeuvres, very good hors d'oeuvres, and they would have drinks which your father would make. And for that half hour the world could be going to hell all around, which it usually was with you kids, but they always stopped and had a drink in these very fine glasses which your mother still has."

"They were very civilized people," Mark interjected, and I recall the three of us laughing uproariously.

"Of course, you can't forget the whole environment," said Mark, "since so many of us were under the gun. The cohesion that took place in that community in which we were so isolated was a very heightening kind of factor. We spent a lot of time with each other because we were kind of isolated, we had the same outlook on life and the same kinds of attitudes and interests and we were in opposition to a lot of things together that were happening."

Probably it was the Gellers' descriptions of the chaos and tensions in that house—the excavation of that part of our lives—that, as much as anything, led me to abandon the book and sent me scurrying back to the safer precincts of conventional journalism, into television, which at the last moment had seemed preferable to going back to the paper.

"The whole confusion in your house was on a personal basis, forget the politics," Mark said, "because—"

"I don't think you can divorce the two," I said.

"Oh yes you can, absolutely"—everyone's voice was rising by then, but theirs was as one, drowning me out.

"You find what happened in your house in many houses, and there's no politics in many houses where there's just a lot of confusion and the kids are running rampant and there's no discipline. . . . Okay, things were heightened by other factors, political factors —they were heightened." Mark was speaking.

"There was anarchy in that house, no question about that," said Emily. "When we'd go to your house at night, and sometimes we'd go for dinner after a workday, everybody was screaming and yelling for attention. So obviously you weren't getting enough attention. I don't think it was physical absence; it may have been your mother's total sense of being unable to deal with the situation.

210

"I remember your mother saying once that one of the biggest mistakes she made in her life was to go back from the West Coast," Emily said. Everyone told me that. In California Estelle Brisker had said, "We all had a sense of mission—a mission which was a grand mission. It was a very happy time." But my mother was pregnant, my father had shipped out, she wanted to be near her mother . . .

Yet surely she knew that Washington was no place for people like my father and her. She would have sensed the danger because she grew up there, just as I somehow always intuited it, even as I rebelled against the fact. But my father would never have comprehended this, nor would anyone who grew up in a place where the clash of ideas and cultures and values is the stuff of everyday existence. There is a code in Washington that you don't break.

She would have recognized that there was trouble ahead, would have felt it in the joints of her knees on those unspeakably humid days on the picket line, certainly *she knew* that to have joined the Communist Party could be ruinous, but more than that she would have known that the whole adventure was going to exact some terrible cost; the evidence is right there on her FBI application after high school, the very act of it. That is the index of her real instincts. J. Edgar Hoover of Seward Square went to Central High, too—he understood; it is no accident that he is the only native of our city to have left an indelible mark on the life of his country.

My father would have understood none of this, but my mother knows the streets and alleys of the District of Columbia, and except for that brief time on the Coast, she has played in them all her life and knows to look both ways before crossing. By 1947 she would have felt trapped between what she believed in and what she understood. For every bold step forward she or my father took, she would have felt even then that they were also marching toward catastrophe.

"There was no precedent in law for the Attorney General's list," my father was saying. "The order created a list of proscribed organizations.

"Emily gave a couple of stupid answers—it's easy to see now. About the Bookshop. She formally quit the Bookshop and said she wasn't using the Bookshop because it wasn't handy. She volunteered the information that she had read that it was subversive.

"The business about the Bookshop was that it was a cultural organization, a meeting place for people who were interested in cultural activities as distinguished from truly political," my father said.

"As far as the kind of activities it was engaged in, it was nothing. I think you'll find a lot of that pattern in the files: union, Bookshop. Because the FBI didn't have anything else. Most of the organizations on the subversive list weren't membership organizations. I've got a feeling that's why Bookshop was important—you got a card. It was a list of left-wing people, of liberals, one of the few the government had—and they went after the membership list.

"The League against War and Fascism—you didn't get a card; you'd go to a meeting and somebody'd put you on a mailing list.

"This business was about a lot of 'front organizations.' I'm using their language. These were almost all organizations that existed before the war, a year or two before, which challenged fascism in various ways."

Creations of the Party? I asked.

"That's where I think it's basically wrong. I think they were premature antifascist." He struggled with the thought: "They didn't equate the dangers in Europe—they didn't equate Russia with Germany. And they weren't opposed to—They were against the rise of fascism and they said that, and they saw Germany and Italy as the spreaders of fascism."

"You're not being articulate," I said, impatient again at his reluctance to tread near the subject of the Communist Party and the Soviet Union.

He snapped back, "People who were usually opposed to fascism,

212

they didn't have to demonstrate they were also opposed to the Soviet Union. I'm trying to figure out why they were on the list. The only reason I can figure out is that their guns were pointed at the growth of the fascist movement and not directed toward Communism."

By 1968, when I went on active duty in the Army, there were still more than one hundred organizations on the Attorney General's list, which I was handed with my paperwork at Fort Benning. "Are you now or have you ever been a member of, or been associated with persons known to you as," etc., etc., the form said.

I checked the box next to the name of the shule, and a few others, noted that I was a reporter and said I had attended all sorts of meetings. It did not keep me out of the Army.

Chapter 26

My father had brought with him to New York three books he was reading: the second volume of Edmund Wilson's journals, a mystery, and a recent biography, *Secrecy and Power: The Life of J. Edgar Hoover,* by Richard Gid Powers; I had postponed reading it, perhaps because the reviews had characterized it as sympathetic to Hoover. "There's a lot of interesting stuff in here," my father said to me.

> Searching for spies [Powers writes] and persuading the government to act against them were only part of Hoover's internal security activities in early 1946. Another was to have plans ready in case he was called upon, in an outbreak of hostilities or of public hysteria, to arrest enemy sympathizers. This cold war "Custodial Detention Program" entailed such elaborate preparations and posed such enormous legal and political risks that it affected almost everything Hoover did in domestic intelligence during the Truman administration. In fact, making the complicated legal, logistical, and political arrangements necessary in order to be able to round up suspects is the thread that connects the seemingly unrelated parts of Hoover's wide-ranging security operations during the cold war. . . .

Planning a detention program and compiling lists of those to be arrested based on their beliefs, and associations, was a major part of the Bureau's intelligence work during the 1940s and 1950s. Hoover's Palmer raids had been derailed, and Palmer's reputation destroyed because not every detail of the dragnets had been worked out ahead of time. Hoover's memory of that disaster fully explains his meticulousness in planning his cold war detention programs.

On June 2, 1919, a bomb destroyed part of the home of Attorney General Mitchell Palmer in Washington. The blast, the mystery of which was never solved, provoked the Justice Department's 1919 drive against radicals, and launched the FBI career (as head of the Bureau's Radical Division) of J. Edgar Hoover. My grandmother remembered the Palmer raids, and the explosion, which she could feel above the tailor shop. The explosion killed the bomb-thrower, and in the rubble police found a leaflet, signed "The Anarchist Fighters," which threatened violence against the "capitalist class." Palmer, claiming he had certain information that there was soon to be an "attempt to rise up and destroy the government at one fell swoop," asked Congress for an unprecedented appropriation to investigate radicals and devised as his strategy a mass roundup and deportation of alien radicals. Hoover was placed in charge of the drive, in which six thousand arrest warrants were issued against foreign-born "anarchists," and deportation proceedings begun against four thousand. This drive to cleanse America of alien "Bolsheviks" and others with "Communist tendencies" bogged down with growing charges against Hoover and Palmer—for violating the rights and due process of those arrested, for manufacturing evidence and inventing a red scare. In the end, fewer than a thousand were deported. "By showing the public the enormous discrepancy between the Justice Department's propaganda about the Communist threat and the pathetic and harmless individuals Hoover had rounded up, . . . the fundamental gap between the plausible theory and the cruel fact of the Red Scare" was exposed, Powers' biography notes.

After my mother testified before the Un-American Committee in 1954, my grandmother decided it was essential that she and my grandfather become American citizens. She studied English, the Constitution, American history; and the day she went down to the Federal Courthouse to take the oath of citizenship was, I think, the proudest day of her life.

For many of my adolescent years I had heard friends of the family react with fury and fear at the prospect of being swept up in an anti-left-wing dragnet in the middle of the night, and if there was a single index to their paranoia and the excess of their rhetoric, it seemed always to me that this particular vision was the jumping-off point, the end of radicalism and the beginning of lunacy.

As evidence that such preparations were in place, these people would invariably cite the Communist Control Act of 1954 (sponsored, my father always pointed out, by the liberal Senator from Minnesota, Hubert H. Humphrey), which indeed gave the government authority to detain not only suspected members of the Communist Party in the event of a national emergency, but also those associated with them or with any of the organizations on the Attorney General's list of subversive organizations. By then the Attorney General's list had become the basis for a whole body of repressive law aimed not only at Communists but also at their "associates" and "sympathizers."

I do not think either of my parents ever believed that the actual apparatus for such a sweep really existed. My father's citation of Humphrey's role in this business had less to do with its substance than with what he regarded as definitive evidence of Humphrey's betrayal of principle—a view he held with perhaps more vehemence than any other political evaluation I have ever heard him make, save for that of Truman and his Loyalty Order.

In fact, one of the distinctions in my mind between the views of my parents and those of their friends was precisely my parents' refusal to believe that somewhere rolls of barbed wire were being readied and put into place in some gulag on the plains.

Thus today whenever I encounter the rubber-stamped entry

216

"DET-COM" (for Detain/Communist) or "RETAIN FOR SECURITY INDEX" in the FBI files of my parents, it infuriates me all the more, incites me.

There are dozens of such notations in their files, dating back to 1941, and Hoover's biographer is right; for this seems to be the primary reason my father and mother continued to be investigated year in and year out, there never being any additional substantive information developed on their activities. Yet with each internal review of their files, exactly such draconian instructions were entered, often accompanied by a buck slip with a penciled checkmark next to the name of Hoover himself or one of his principal assistants.

> BERNSTEIN, ALFRED DAVID: This case has been re-evaluated in the light of the Security Index criteria and it continues to fall within such criteria . . .
>
> Subject has continued activities in CP front groups and his activities and associations depict the subject as an individual who could be expected to commit acts inimical to the National Defense and public safety of the U.S. in time of emergency.

By the time I had gotten the FBI files I already realized dimly that the apparatus for detaining my parents and others really existed, and that on at least one occasion the first motions had apparently been taken—in 1962, during the Cuban missile crisis.

There had been a series of strange phone calls on the second or third day of the crisis, answered by me or my sisters, each caller asking for our parents: did we know when they would return home, were they out of town, did they have any plans to be away from home that week?

That evening my parents had invited a dozen old friends from the union days for dinner, to watch television accounts of the drama. I arrived after work at the *Star* and mentioned that there had been an odd call that morning; my sisters then told of receiving similar calls; and it developed that almost all the people eating off TV trays and trying to fathom what was happening between Kennedy and

Khrushchev had also received strange calls of some sort that day, all trying to fix their whereabouts for the coming week.

Even then, I was reluctant to embrace the outraged conclusion of everyone else in that room. But that moment, I know, was an awakening for me, the first time I was forced to consider that the paranoid vision of these people might not be so paranoid—that the nightmare apparitions of my childhood were not without foundation, and that perhaps I should pay a bit more attention to what my parents and their friends had told me.

> During the Truman administration [writes Richard Gid Powers], Hoover had accomplished what he had tried—and failed—to do during the Palmer raids. This time he was armed with the prestige acquired over his long career, together with the peacetime sedition law he lacked in 1920, a series of spectacular loyalty cases and an international emergency that produced a need and a demand for action against the disloyal.
>
> The internal security issue that shook and eventually destroyed the Truman administration was a symptom of a fundamental reordering of the American political consciousness. The search for spies, the hunt for disloyal government officials, the extirpation of the Communist party in the courts of law during the early years of the cold war were all part of a struggle to redefine the limits of political respectability. He had at last been able to place the authority of the government behind his drive to make the values of Seward Square the official morality of the nation.

The relevant papers, I learned, are to be found in the Truman Library:

> Pres feels very strongly anti FBI & sides positively with Mitchell and Perkins. [This was noted on May 2, 1947, by Truman's military aide, George Elsey. Harry B. Mitchell was chairman of the Civil Service Commission, and Frances Perkins, the former Secretary of Labor, was a Commission member.]
>
> Wants to be sure and hold FBI down, afraid of "Gestapo."
>
> Pres came in twice to CMC's office on 1st May to express these views.

218

What Truman had come into Clark M. Clifford's office to express were his views that the whole loyalty program should not be turned over lock, stock, and barrel to J. Edgar Hoover, as the FBI Director was demanding. Initially it had been proposed by the President (and his Temporary Commission on Loyalty) that the Civil Service Commission establish investigative machinery to handle loyalty inquiries about prospective employees of the government, and that the FBI —which already had conducted loyalty investigations of incumbent employees under other statutes—continue to investigate only those already in the work force.

Clifford warned the President that Congress would probably object and insist that the FBI control the whole program. On the bottom of a memo from Clifford, Truman jotted: "Clark, you have properly diagnosed the case. But J. Edgar will in all probability get this backward looking Congress to give him what he wants. It's dangerous. HST."

Truman agreed to Clifford's recommendation that he accede to the FBI's demands.

Philip Murray of the CIO wrote to Truman asking that the order be repealed unless it could be made to comply with due process, citing the absence of a definition of disloyalty and its lack of a guarantee that the accused person could confront his or her accusers and cross-examine witnesses. "Murray's letter," Robert Donovan writes in his biography of Truman, "raised the essential question, as important now as then: Are there to be democracy and constitutional freedoms at all times? Or in times of danger, real or imagined, must free expression and constitutional procedures be modified, thus subtly changing the system while trying to preserve it?"

"The order," Truman replied to Phil Murray, "was carefully drawn with the idea in view that the Civil Rights of no one would be infringed upon and its administration will be carried out in that spirit."

Chapter 27

Emily Geller's hearing was in two parts; my father requested the second one, to consider new evidence, after the board had found against her on September 9, 1948. In the first hearing, the record shows, there was nothing to support the charge of disloyalty; the board members had been presented with forty-one affidavits asserting the implausibility and groundlessness of the charges. By the second hearing my father was able to determine with considerable certainty how the charges (of CP membership, of underground activity, of favoritism to union members) came to be developed and substantiated in the FBI's investigation. If there was a single loyalty case handled by my father in which it was alleged that the accused actually took part in any activity directly aimed at undermining the government of the United States (or its authority), I have been unable to find it. Nor was a single loyalty case based on substantiated activities undertaken as a member of the Communist Party, as far as I can determine.

It amazes me how close to the truth my father was able to come, unaided, in those days as he undertook to defend Emily Geller and the hundreds of other government employees who came through our dining room. There was no Freedom of Information Act then, and there were few journalistic tools to loosen the vise of secrecy and collusion, the daisy chain of G-men and congressional spycatchers and sleuths. He chose as witnesses government officials who had moved from the New Deal agencies into the most security-conscious branches of federal service after the war: the CIA, the Defense Department, the Atomic Energy Commission. These were individuals who had undergone the most rigorous loyalty investigations of all.

In Emily's case, he called the chief classification officer at the National Institutes of Health, who gave her an unequivocally positive evaluation and said he knew of nothing she had ever said or done that suggested "Communistic" leanings or bias.

"Is there anything else you want to tell the Board?" my father asked.

"Yes, I would like to mention something that came up. There is a Mr. Kilgore among my acquaintances at the National Institutes of Health. I know Kilgore as an acquaintance. I have been to his house to play bridge. And Kilgore made a derogatory statement one day. He inferred she was with the Communist bunch at OPA. . . ."

"Did he give you any proof?"

"I asked him why? That if she was a communist, I wanted to know. The only two things he mentioned was her membership in the union, which I did not consider would make her a communist, and the fact that she had, in his opinion, been biased in serving union people."

"Was it Kilgore's statement that she was a rabid unionite?" my father asked.

"Yes, we checked a little more carefully than we do in most cases, because of that statement."

". . . What was the reaction you got?"

"I got very excellent recommendations. Every recommendation I got was excellent. People praised her ability and her previous work record."

"Did you get any reports that reflected unfavorably on her loyalty to the United States?" my father asked.

"None," the witness answered.

"Can you identify for the Board Manley Kilgore?" my father asked Dallas Johnson, chief of Cancer Reports at the National Institutes of Health.

"Yes, I can. He is an administrative officer in the Cancer Grants Section. I don't know, I dislike him so much, maybe I can't—does this have any bearing on this?"

"Will you tell the Board why you dislike him?"

"I had to work for a week with him, at which time he was quite obnoxious to me personally," she said. "I don't mean— I know that in mobs there are people that you sometimes don't get along with. But he was obnoxious. I dislike him. He was pursuing me and I didn't like it. He was drunk a great deal of the time. He drinks. He was arrested a year ago. That is generally known."

My father then presented a photostat of the front page of the *Washington Post* of December 26, 1947, reporting Mr. Kilgore's arrest for disorderly conduct and drunkenness. "I would also like to state that the records of the Municipal Court for the District of Columbia further reveal that on February 5, 1948, Mr. Kilgore was charged with drunkenness and forfeited his bond," he told the board.

He tracked down the members of Manley Kilgore's car pool. "It was a somewhat unreliable car pool, because he was apt to take off from the office and not come back," one of the young women testified. "And one day he did drive us home when it was very icy and Manley was not fit to drive; he had been drinking. It was too much for me and the other girls. We all quit that night; we said we wouldn't be riding with him anymore."

"He is just sort of a weak character," Dallas Johnson concluded. "I don't suppose he can help it." She had been a reporter for *The New York Times* before coming to the National Cancer Institute at NIH. "It was very rough in the first year because there was no one in the Classification Section who knew what I was trying to do," she testified. "My joy and affection for Mrs. Geller started when she

222

came in and in a day and a half she wrote up 123 jobs. . . . In setting up those jobs she did a fair and intelligent job. It was really a great joy to work with her.''

Emily was on the fast track.

"I would say that Mrs. Geller's reputation was of being the most intelligent and capable of the junior people who had come into the agency. I know the impression was universal," another supervisor, from OPA, testified.

"I would have been one of the three people in charge of Personnel for NIH," Emily said to me recently, in Washington. "That's where I was headed—that was what I wanted to do with my professional life."

Gorbachev had just arrived in Washington, and the television was on. My mother was in the kitchen cooking dinner. My father was in Atlantic City; he goes once a month or so, sets himself a limit of three hundred dollars and usually comes out ahead at the crap table. He always takes the bus.

"Don't you think your mother and I should have been invited to the reception at the embassy?" Emily said to me when I came through the door.

She affected a hurt smile, and laughed, but I could tell there was a piece of her that wasn't altogether kidding—beneath the laughter, some sense of dues paid. "After all, we were for this, an end to the Cold War, forty years ago."

Recently she had been in Russia: she and two hundred other Americans had marched from Leningrad to Moscow in the cause of world peace. "This nonsense," my father had described the endeavor to me in a private moment, and he rolled his eyes a bit. Mark had stayed at home in Los Angeles.

My mother, I think, was a little envious; clearly she was quite taken with the idea of Emily sleeping in a tent somewhere out there on the Soviet steppes, and the two of them were giggling like a couple of girls, more like sisters actually, for that is exactly how they are together. Emily described her backpack and its contents, explaining that she had sewn in her own name tags.

"They do have Velcro nowadays," my mother said.

That night as I was leaving I asked Emily how she felt about what had happened in those years, now that she better understood the forces and procedures arrayed against her. She had at last gotten her FBI file: the Reagan Administration had been trying to curtail the Freedom of Information Act—too many secrets were getting out, the Attorney General, Mr. Meese, maintained.

"I wouldn't have done anything differently, given the circumstances," she said. "It was important to fight—to take a stand. I like being a social worker today; I think it was rougher on Mark, it was harder for him to find work." The only allegation against Mark that was substantial was that he had married Emily; everything else was refuted.

My father had won his case. A few months later a new set of charges was filed against him. Rather than face another loyalty hearing, he quit the government.

In 1985 Emily was selected for appointment by the Governor of California to serve on the state board that oversees the practice of psychiatric social workers there.

She declined after consulting with my father. "It would have required an investigation," she said. "One of the questions was whether I was ever the subject of a loyalty investigation; they would have wanted the information in the FBI files.

"I just didn't want to go through it all again at this age," she said.

Chapter 28

My father put Emily on the stand and asked her whether she had succeeded Olivia Abelson or Olivia Israeli or anybody else as secretary of the government underground group of the Communist Party.

"No," she answered.

"At this time," he told the board, "I would like to present a photostat of a Certificate of Birth Registration issued by the Health Department of the District of Columbia. The certificate shows that Mrs. Abelson gave birth to a child in December 1945, so she wasn't pregnant in April 1946 as alleged."

No point was left unaddressed.

The examiner resumed, "Again reverting back to question number two, which states your reasons for becoming a member of the Southern Conference on Human Welfare, I wonder if we might have that, Mrs. Geller."

It is difficult to characterize the fascinating monotony of this document, with its rhythmic incantations of names and events and associations, each tinged sinister, its cover page blue: *Regional Loyalty Board Hearing on Supplemental Interrogatory in the Case of Mrs.*

Emily Ann Geller, held on April 20, 1949 in Room 1220 of Temporary Building R, Washington, D.C.

Temporary Building R was at Twelfth Street, across from the Smithsonian Castle. The "tempos" were ugly single-story huts of asbestos siding that were erected on both sides of the Mall to contain the work force of bursting wartime Washington. They were finally torn down during the Kennedy administration. It was not until the Kennedy administration that the government began to recover from the effects of the loyalty purge, my father says—that the intellectual climate of government again became receptive to some diversity of thought and opinion.

The first time I ever observed the green sweep of the entire Mall was from the Lincoln Memorial, on August 28, 1963, dawn, as the first marchers gathered. By noontime the entire Mall was filled all the way to the Capitol, and Martin Luther King spoke his dream.

"Well, as a member of minority groups, I have always been very much interested in the protection of the minority groups, and the Southern Conference for Human Welfare seemed to be an organization that was concerned with the problem and was attempting to do something about the problem," Emily Geller testified on an April afternoon in 1949. "I was interested in such problems as poll tax and suffrage. The President's Committee on Civil Rights had just published their report, or preliminary statements, and it seemed to me a good organization to belong to."

It is clear from the record that the members of the loyalty board wished to make an issue of the fact the Emily Geller had changed her maiden name from Levin to Lewis.

Noting that she had changed her name from a Jewish one to a Gentile-sounding one, a board member saw an inconsistency: "Mrs. Geller, you said, I believe, that you joined this Society for Human Welfare because you were interested in minority groups, meaning you identified with one of them yourself. . . . Well, why did you change your name from Levin to Lewis, which in the former name you would be identified and in the latter name you would not?"

"Because my brother, of whom I was very fond, had also changed

226

his name," Emily said. After she had been charged with disloyalty, her brother did not speak to her for twelve years.

"Will you explain your residence, Mrs. Geller, who tenanted the place, and what sort of setup you had?" "What are the names of these individuals you said you resided with? . . . What sort of work did they do?" ("They were economists, I think . . . two sisters, twin sisters, one was at Treasury and the other one was with a war agency, the War Production Board, I think.") "Where did Audrey Beller work? . . . Do you recall a Rhoda Epstein living with you in the apartment or visiting you at the apartment? . . . Do you recall the name of Janette Gaines Stern?" ("I've never heard of her.") "Were there other individuals in the apartment besides the ones you have named—in the apartment building with whom you were rather closely associated?" ("Yes, I was friendly with a boy that I had met in the union who also lived in the apartment house. . . . He was working in the War Department when I first met him and then he transferred to the OPA. And then he went into the Army and I never saw him after that.") ". . . Did you ever reside at this address with anyone who is presently associated with the California Labor Schools? . . . Did you have any particular reason for leaving that apartment?" ("It wasn't a good apartment. We didn't have a kitchen and it was only one room and it was very hot in the summer.")

Despite its more repellent aspects, the record of Emily Geller's hearing is a wondrous document of the real concerns and activities of people like her, people whose names are typed on the index tabs in the files kept in the basement and under the steps in Silver Spring. Names to the FBI, to the Loyalty Boards. People to me. *Progressive People*, as I had first chosen to call the book.

I had started out skeptical: my initial perceptions (formed as a child and carried into adulthood) were that the Communist Party and its actions were the reason for their ordeal, for the loyalty order and for much of what had happened to the country. I was wrong.

227

Between 1947 and 1954, more than eight thousand people were accused and driven from the government under Executive Order 9835.

The Loyalty Order, and the Attorney General's list, amended over the years, were not rescinded until 1974, in the wake of Watergate.

In those files, I came to realize, was the hidden history of our times: beneath the steps in Silver Spring the real stuff of our epoch had been preserved.

Emily Geller's case was not the worst.

Recently I got a call from a friend on the Coast, someone I've known for fifteen years. "I hear your book is almost finished," she said. "I've been waiting a long time for this book." I joked that I had, too, but then she told me that her father had been the subject of a loyalty hearing in 1949 and had lost his job as a clerk for the Patent Office in New York. He died not long after. "He never got over it; and neither did my mother" she said. "This is the first I've ever talked about what happened."

A scholar in Massachusetts, who had tried for a decade to get publishers interested in the subject, wrote to me. She had been in touch with Marie Siegrist and asked whether I could send her the file of Marie's loyalty hearings. Later, she told me of some of the cases she had unearthed. I had read through perhaps a hundred others that my father had singled out.

A former member of Congress, a lawyer, told me how the whole of the organized bar, and even most of the civil-rights lawyers of the day, had been willing to take cases only if the accused could demonstrate that they had never even remotely been involved in causes espoused by the left.

At the Truman Library the keeper of the President's papers told me, "I always wondered when someone would get around to this."

Chapter 29

On February 7, 1949, the Executive secretary of the loyalty board had written to J. Edgar Hoover about the case of Emily Geller.

> By way of background [an FBI summary prepared for Hoover begins], the Emily Ann Geller case has been remanded by the Loyalty Review Board to the Fourth Civil Service Loyalty Board on two occasions. Mrs. Geller is being defended by Al Bernstein . . . Bernstein has consistently requested very detailed information in the letters of charges and the Fourth Civil Service Loyalty Board has refused to furnish him any detailed data. . . .

The board, it developed, met secretly a few weeks later with a personal emissary from Hoover, and was furnished with a letter from the Director that casts considerable light on how the government's allegations came to be made in these loyalty cases.

> Confidential informants [deleted] and [deleted] are both reliable and are in a position to have knowledge concerning the information which they have furnished [Hoover wrote the board]. These

two confidential informants, upon reinterview, have both advised that they cannot definitely state from records or other documents that the appointee is a member and general secretary of the Communist Party underground but these informants have personal knowledge of an established pattern of association by appointee with persons whom these informants know to be members of the Communist Party. This association by appointee has indicated to these informants, who are familiar with Communist Party activities, that appointee is secretary of the Communist Party underground group.

In their meeting with the FBI, according to Hoover's emissary, members of the loyalty board asked what was meant by "established pattern."

I advised . . . the board that the two informants who had previously furnished us information were familiar with Communist Party activities and the activities of the appointee, and that their observations of the appointee lead [sic] them to believe that she was the general secretary of the Communist Party underground.

I further stressed . . . that for me to give more detailed data as to exactly what activities formed this pattern the identity of the informants would be jeopardized. I also impressed the fact that all members of the Communist Party underground operate very "sub rosa" and that in compliance with specific instructions issued by the Communist Party they are extremely careful to conceal any activities promoting the communist cause.

Mr. Norris and Mr. Blair [of the loyalty board] thanked the writer for these observations.

RECOMMENDATION: None. This is for record purposes.

If for no other reason, history should be grateful (at this late hour) that Hoover's m.o. included a mania for record-keeping and the preservation of the Bureau's files.

"Did the FBI question you about Mrs. Geller?" my father asked Irvin Rice, Emily's boss at OPA.

230

"Yes. I was asked if there had occurred anything on any of those occasions which would lead me to the conclusion that Mrs. Geller was disloyal. I obviously answered no."

My father asked whether there had been anything unusual about the FBI's questioning.

"The questioning stood out, as I recall it, because it is probably the longest interview I had had with a member of the FBI, and in my position as administrator of the Sugar Rationing Branch I had frequent contacts with them, so I generally know how the routine of questions go. . . . It is my personal opinion, of course, but I got the impression that the investigator was hoping that I would say more than I had said; that probably I was not telling him the things he hoped to hear. But I gave him all the information that was available to me and everything that I knew. Beyond that I couldn't give him any more."

MR. MARTIN [a board member]: Let me ask you this further question. You don't think that if a person was a communist and that person were in the Government employ and had gotten there or been placed there by the Communist Party and that person was in a position to do the Communist Party some good, or would give them information or exercise some influence that would be helpful to the Communist Party, you don't think that this person would openly associate with other communists, do you? Couldn't Mrs. Geller influence others in that department if she were clever enough . . . without stirring up any publicity or creating any undue attention to herself . . . ?

WITNESS: If you are asking me if I see a ghost standing in the doorway: It may be there; I can't see it.

MR. MARTIN: Well, a person who wanted to operate cleverly wouldn't use pressure! Wouldn't they use intrigue and suave methods rather than pressure? The point I am trying to make is this: A person who is actually a Communist may outwardly exhibit every symptom or every characteristic to others of being a loyal American, yet he might be the most zealous Communist but may be able to conceal his feelings to the extent that no one other than Communists with whom he associates may know that fact.

231

"In summation here," my father began, "what are the facts in this case really?"

His language is drawn from the handwritten notes I found in another file, the script surprisingly neat, bold strokes of the pen on every other line of the yellow legal paper.

(I like to touch the sheets of paper, can imagine him holding them as he stands and then paces back and forth: Yesterday I called him to tell him that Jacob, my older son, had come upstairs to ask me whether I paced when I worked. "Yes," I said—in fact, I was walking between the typewriter and the fireplace at the time. "So do I; I think better when I pace," Jacob said—he is nine—and went back to his homework after he had talked on the phone to his grandfather.)

"Briefly the facts are that Mrs. Geller entered the Government Service about seven years ago fresh out of college as a low-grade statistic clerk and, as a result of further academic training, hard work and ability, has risen in service to a point where she now occupies a responsible position in the Personnel Office of the Public Health Service. . . . She has earned the respect of co-workers and supervisors."

He pronounced "groundless" the charge that Emily had infiltrated Communists into the government and noted that "recruitment of personnel did not even come within her jurisdiction.

"I really don't know as her counsel how to get at the charge that she is a member of the Communist Party, or Secretary of an Underground Group of the Communist Party," he confessed. "There is no foundation to that charge. We wish there were some more specific information so that we could deny it in specific terms. We have done the best we could in view of the kind of information that we have been given by the Board. . . .

"As far as the charge that she is the Secretary of the Communist Underground, that really borders on the fantastic."

There is a cadence to his words, a certain meter:

"That is important because it brings us to the crux of the case. At the time that it was alleged that she was the secretary of this so-

232

called Underground she was a Secretary of an organization—it was a matter of public record, she didn't hide it, she wasn't secretive about it. That organization was her local union. I don't think, Gentlemen, that this is a loyalty case. It all revolves around the fact that Mrs. Geller has been an active union member and leader for a good many years.

"I want to point out that the union she has been affiliated with is not on any subversive list of the Attorney General. I want to point out that it is recognized by this Government and has been for ten years; that while this proceeding is going on, other officials are engaging in negotiations throughout the Government on matters of employer–employee relationships and that it is one of the largest, if not the largest, of the government employee unions.

"I noticed quite a few references were made to various people who have been active in our union, such as Arthur Stein, Donald Murray, Henry Beitscher"—he was the one with the lapel pin. "I don't know the basis of these innuendoes," my father said, "but I do know that Arthur Fleming is much better acquainted with Arthur Stein and Donald Murray than Mrs. Geller is." Fleming was the chairman of the Civil Service Commission at the time.

Arthur Stein was my father's closest friend. He was on his way to meet my father for lunch, in 1961, when he died. My father went to the morgue and identified his body.

"Only once during my hearing do I recall getting angry at your father," Emily told me. She and Dad and Artie Stein had been walking back from lunch to the union office, on Ninth Street, across from where the Martin Luther King Library is today. Suddenly my father and Artie disappeared, vanished. Finally she spotted the neon pinball sign of the penny arcade and, inside, Dad and Artie side by side at two machines, smiles of contentment across their faces.

My father's pinball style is calm, measured, even elegant. He waits for the ball, lets it take its own course, then gently flips it in the desired direction. My own style is very much the opposite, and not a little showy; I shake the machine until it almost tilts, seek the maximum momentum and let the ball career unpredictably, though finally I'll slow it down until I can balance it on the flipper and take my best shot—hard.

"It is irritating, to say the least, to come here and on the basis of I don't know what to quiz a rank-and-file Government employee and a rank-and-file member of your union because of her relationship with officials of this union while these officials are on a day-to-day relationship with the highest officials of the Government," my father told the loyalty board. "This is not a subversive organization that we are talking about, this is a union.

"I don't think her activities in the union are a proper subject for a loyalty investigation. If she has abused her office, because of union affiliations, there is a procedure which should be utilized. That is rule number ten of the Civil Service Commission Act. Let us assume that she has abused her office for the purpose of doing something or other for the union; is that saying that she is treasonous? Is that saying that she is disloyal to her Government?"

"There is no such intimation in the hearing that I know of," the chairman interrupted.

The examiner joined the protest. "We did not question her activities in the union—"

"That was merely an incident in the investigation," said another member of the board (not mentioning that it was the basis for the endless fishing expedition through apartments and roommates and faceless names).

"Well, what I want to show is that her relationship with these people is no different than that of the highest of Government officials. . . . I am trying to give the Board information which will clear up the matter of association, why she associates with these people. *I know of no other way of doing it except by hitting back. . . .*"

I cannot discern from the record whether my father's aggressive tack helped or hurt the situation. "As I say, it is very difficult to

234

determine why you ask these questions. I have to make these guesses in order to protect her, I think." He spoke of a procedure in which Emily "could be deprived of her ability to earn a living . . . that could ruin her reputation and that of her family in the community because she has been active in the union."

"Understand this," responded the chairman, "the only point we are getting at is whether or not she has knowingly associated with Communists. That was the basic thing and if she says she doesn't know any Communists and has never associated with Communists anywhere in the union, or out of the union, that is her answer."

"The very charge that she belongs to a Communist-dominated union—you are right away throwing a lot of paint all over the real situation," my father asserted.

"We haven't charged Mrs. Geller with anything," the examiner retorted. "That is something that you are reading into it."

"Well, as I understand your procedure, your interrogatory is in effect a series of charges," my father noted.

"We are not charging her," the examiner insisted. "We say that information has been received that she has been a member of a union that has been infiltrated and dominated by the Communists, and we have asked her to explain. . . ."

My father noted again that the union was not on the Attorney General's list of subversive organizations. Nor, for that matter, was the Southern Conference for Human Welfare.

"Maybe I don't understand the function of the Attorney General's list stating the organizations which are considered to be subversive. This seems to be a device: just using the term 'Communist-dominated' you get at the same step."

Back and forth. Back and forth.

It is a strange way to get to know your father, reading between these lines, looking for his words in exchanges with government lawyers, congressmen, senators, examiners, committee counsels.

MR. BERNSTEIN: Let me tell you how I view it. I view this situation as charges that would come from a particular agency, that you

235

are government by the Executive Order, and under the Order you use the form and devices, and the interrogatory is the form you use for the set of charges—it occupies the same place.

MR. CHAIRMAN: You can play upon words all you wish, my dear sir, I have told you what the situation is.

And Emily Geller told the loyalty board, "I hope that you view these affidavits very seriously with regard to the charges. The witnesses and the affidavits from people who are in a position to view my work over a period of years, who know everything that I did during a period of years, should be weighed very carefully against the word of certain individuals, one of whom has been named, I think, who out of sheer malice or sheer personal dislike at not getting what he wanted, attempted to deface my loyalty and character. And at the same time, I think, the affidavits not only point that out, but also point out the groundlessness of the one specific charge as to how I used my office in terms of time spent, and what kind of a person I am.

"All the charges grieve me very much," she said. "They astound me and grieve me."

"Do you think you have had a fair hearing, Mrs. Geller?"

This was the last question, asked by the chairman.

"Well, I think it has been a fair hearing," she answered finally. "I have been a little confused by the first set of charges and the second set, particularly the relationship between the two." The second set of charges, enumerated in the supplemental interrogatory, had been added when my father sought a new hearing: her alleged association with Annie Stein, Betty Hayes and the others, and her reputed attendance at a Bookshop picnic and a lecture at the Bookshop. "Other than that, I think it has been a fair hearing."

"I have nothing further to say," my father concluded.

I imagine him worn down, spent, dejected.

"I would like the Board to reconsider this case and let us know its determination as expeditiously as possible."

236

Chapter 30

"Mr. Bernstein, did you protest this Loyalty Order? Were you one of those that protested the President's Executive order?"

My father was asked this by Representative Clare Hoffman, Republican of Michigan, on February 28, 1948.

"I don't quite get what you mean," my father said.

He was under oath. The ostensible reason for his being on the witness stand was the strike by the government cafeteria workers— for higher wages and the right to organize. The House Committee on Education and Labor had decided to investigate whether Communists were behind it.

That morning, the day after my sister Mary's first birthday, federal marshals had shown up at the union office and hauled away all the union's records. Congressman Hoffman had specifically directed them to seize the Addressograph plates listing all its members.

The union office was at 930 F Street. A disco called the 930 Club occupies the building today.

"You know, the President has an order called the Loyalty Order," the Congressman said.

"Let me tell you about that," my father responded. "My personal opinion on the Loyalty Order, I think it is a deprivation of fundamental civil liberties."

"To ask any federal employee to declare his loyalty?"

"No."

"What, then, do you object to?"

"I object to the procedures involved in this matter."

"You do not think it is improper?"

"I think any man who is accused of a terrible charge, like disloyalty, which to my mind is on a par with treason, should have his day in court, and the procedure under Executive Order 9835 certainly does not give it to him."

"Do you not think that anyone accused of such a terrible charge should be happy to have the opportunity to deny it?"

"He cannot have the opportunity to deny it when he does not get specific charges or the right to confront his accusers, or have a determination by an impartial body. . . . Here is a procedure which permits a man on the rolls who might have been there for eighteen years—and, by the way, I know of a case where a man . . . was in there twelve years, and some crackpot accused him of disloyalty, and he never had a chance to meet his accusers, and he never had a chance to defend himself, and he never had specific charges, and he is carrying that stigma around with him for the rest of his life, and he cannot get employment.

"That is what I have got against this business. That is not American."

MR. HOFFMAN: Suppose you say to me, "Hoffman, you are a thief."

MR. BERNSTEIN: I would not say that.

MR. HOFFMAN: Would you not think I would be very anxious and quick to say "You do not know what you are talking about. I am not; I never stole a thing in my life"?

MR. BERNSTEIN: If I said, "Hoffman, you are a thief," you would say "Give me some charges, and give me a chance."

MR. HOFFMAN: The first thing I would do is say "That is not so."

238

MR. BERNSTEIN: Would that prove it?

MR. HOFFMAN: No; but it would be a denial.

MR. BERNSTEIN: You would go around with a stigma of "Bernstein called you a thief," and you would carry that stigma for the rest of your life, and you would not have an opportunity to deny it.

"We all admit all of that," the Congressman responded, and he asked my father, "Do you think the Communists are enemies of our country?"

It could not have been comfortable there at the green baize table, with the photographers and their bright lights, and thoughts of perjury, the Smith Act, contempt of Congress. The object was to avoid taking the Fifth Amendment, if possible—the stigma.

"What do you think of the Communists, and the doctrine they teach, and the party?" the Congressman demanded.

"I think any organization which is engaged in an effort to overthrow our Government by force and violence is a dangerous organization," my father responded.

MR. HOFFMAN: Do you believe in fair play?

MR. BERNSTEIN: Certainly.

MR. HOFFMAN: Will you keep still when I ask you a question?

MR. BERNSTEIN: I am sorry.

MR. HOFFMAN: You think the Loyalty Order is unfair, do you?

MR. BERNSTEIN: I think it is disgraceful as a piece of business.

MR. HOFFMAN: What does that loyalty order require?

MR. BERNSTEIN: It permits a man to be branded disloyal without giving him a fair hearing.

MR. HOFFMAN: That is your conviction of it?

MR. BERNSTEIN: That is the conviction of every decent lawyer in the country, conservative or otherwise.

MR. HOFFMAN: The Government has a right, has it not, to hire whoever it wishes to?

MR. BERNSTEIN: Let me explain how it operates.

MR. HOFFMAN: I know how it operates.

MR. BERNSTEIN: You don't have an opportunity to confront your accuser; that is basic American jurisprudence. . . .

MR. HOFFMAN: You are strong for the Constitution; are you not?
MR. BERNSTEIN: You are right; I am.
MR. HOFFMAN: But you are not interested in an organization which advocates the overthrow of the Government established by the Constitution by force; you just said you were not.
MR. BERNSTEIN: You are misquoting me.
MR. HOFFMAN: I am not misquoting you. . . . You are strong for the Constitution when you want something that the Constitution guarantees, are you not?
MR. BERNSTEIN: I am strong for the Constitution in every instance, and I have a consistent record on it.
MR. HOFFMAN: But when the Government established under that Constitution wants you to declare your loyalty to that Government, then you say that it is wrong.
MR. BERNSTEIN: I have declared my loyalty in no uncertain terms.

And Congressman Hoffman asked him, "What do you think about these radio commentators and these fellows in the paper who are continually accusing Congressmen of a lot of stuff. They have to carry that load around, too. Did you ever think of that?

MR. BERNSTEIN: I think that you boys are able to defend yourself. I would like to be on that side of the table.

Several days before, the committee had announced that it planned hearings into the cafeteria strike and that the top leadership of the union would be called to testify. Anticipating a subpoena, my father and Artie Stein took the train to New York that afternoon. They arrived in Manhattan in the midst of a huge snowstorm—a blizzard, in fact—and could not find a hotel room. Finally they made their way to Hotel One Fifth Avenue; a desk clerk had told them on the phone that a small room was available. The room, however, was occupied when they arrived, soaked and shivering. The clerk instead offered them Artur Rubinstein's vacant penthouse suite.

240

It was a wonderful weekend, my father recalls, with Artie playing "Show Me the Way to Go Home" on Rubinstein's Steinway grand, and the two of them doing some fancy singing while they waited for the blizzard to end and planned how to respond to the investigation of the House Committee on Education and Labor. Finally it was decided that my father would go back to answer the inevitable subpoena while Artie remained in New York.

A few years later, the whole family stayed at the One Fifth Avenue for a week, during an investigation by the House Committee on Un-American Activities. To this day I regard its tower as something of a beacon, welcoming, familiar—and, sometimes when I'm in the Village, I like to stop in the lobby, sit in one of the big green leather chairs, and read the paper.

"The question is, Are you a Communist? That is the question that is up now," another Congressman said.

> MR. BERNSTEIN: That is where you and I disagree.
> CONGRESSMAN SMITH: You think that I have no right as an individual employer, or the Government has no right to ask that of you if you want employment.
> MR. BERNSTEIN: I did not say that at all, sir. I say that your Government has got a perfect right to ask anybody if they are subversive and if somebody is subversive, and he gets a hearing on it, and a fair hearing, and a fair determination, that is something else.

Congressman Hoffman asked him, "Do you think an employer, for instance, a manufacturer of guns that the Army or the Navy wants, should not have the right to ask an applicant for a job to sign an affidavit that he is not a member of the Communist Party?"

> MR. BERNSTEIN: Let me explain how I feel about it.
> MR. HOFFMAN: Just stick to my question, now.
> MR. BERNSTEIN: I am against all affidavits of this type.

241

MR. HOFFMAN: No, no; now, come on and answer the question. Your testimony indicates that you are well educated, and you know what is going on in the world.

"I think there is a witch-hunt going," my father said.

Chapter 31

My father's last political activity of the era was as chairman of the Progressive Party's Anti-Discrimination Committee, in the early fifties. The Progressive Party had been the force behind the efforts, ultimately successful, to desegregate Washington's swimming pools. I had always associated this struggle with my mother, until I found an old clipping. It described the charge of the Park Police cavalry, wielding their batons like polo mallets; that afternoon we had tried to bring black children with us to the pool at West Potomac Park, at Haines Point—Speedway. The story in the *Star* was written by Coit Hendley, Jr. (the editor who had taken me with him to New Jersey), and it quoted my father.

The *Washington Post*'s stories about integration of the pools were written by Benjamin C. Bradlee.

"They were awful people," Bradlee was saying of the Progressive Party.

"Watch it, those are my in-laws," my wife said, and we all laughed. This was at dinner in 1977. I had just left the paper—to do this book. By then, Bradlee knew a fair bit about the family history.

In the mid-sixties, when Bradlee became managing editor of the *Washington Post*, I decided I wanted to work there. I attempted to get hired through the paper's metropolitan editor, and I thought I had succeeded until I received a call in New Jersey from Ben Gilbert, who was by then the deputy managing editor. Could I come down the next day to meet with him?

Gilbert's office was a small cubicle off the newsroom floor, and he shut the door behind me after the secretary had shown me in. Behind his desk, on a console, were pictures of his children, Amy and Ian. Ian was a lawyer now, he said.

We shook hands, and I remembered his awkwardness. He was wearing a polka-dotted silk bow tie.

"How are Mom and Dad?" he asked, and I said fine, and then he got right to the point.

He said that he liked my work and that a decision had been made to hire me. It would be good to have me at the *Post*. For a moment I thought that this visit was his way of clearing the air, of reaching out, and I was not untouched.

"There is one more matter," he said. "Are you political?"

I remember closing my eyes for a moment and then feeling a sense of utter calm settling over me as I calculated my response.

Gilbert himself had come from a left-wing background, had been active on the left at City College in New York. During the witch-hunts he had feared for his job at the *Post*. That, I knew, was why contact had been cut off that day in 1954.

I had some obvious choices, and I like to think now that my answer reflected a bit of each: my rage and disgust, and my desire to be hired, and the hope that I would emerge with some dignity, but I am not entirely sure.

I stood up. "Ben, the only two organizations I've ever belonged to are B'nai B'rith Youth and the Newspaper Guild." I had been a leader in both. I said that if he wanted to hire me, fine, and if he

244

didn't want to hire me, fine, and that I was leaving and going back to New Jersey on the next plane. I shut the door behind me.

I went to work for the *Washington Post* the next week, in October 1966.

On November 3, 1949, a year after Emily Geller was fired, the United States Court of Appeals for the District of Columbia Circuit reviewed the dismissal of Dorothy Bailey from her job as a training supervisor in the U.S. Employment Service. Almost all the charges against her related to her union activities, among them her association with my father. Milt Freeman, my father's old law school chum, handled her case—very ably—with Abe Fortas and Paul Porter and Thurmond Arnold; Milt gave me the file of her proceedings after he and I lunched in 1977 at the Metropolitan Club. Included in the boxes of material was a yellowed copy of Judge Henry W. Edgerton's opinion in the case:

> Without trial by jury, without evidence, and without even being allowed to confront her accusers or to know their identity, a citizen of the United States has been found disloyal to the government of the United States.
>
> For her supposed disloyal thoughts she has been punished. . . . The case received nation-wide publicity. Ostracism inevitably followed. A finding of disloyalty is closely akin to a finding of treason. The public hardly distinguishes between the two.
>
> No charges were served on appellant. The chairman of the Regional Board said, "Nobody has presented any charges." . . . No witness offered evidence, even hearsay evidence, against appellant. No affidavits were introduced against her. Yet the Board purported to find "on all the evidence" that there were reasonable grounds for believing she was disloyal to the government of the United States. . . .
>
> Against all this, there were only the unsworn reports in the secret files [of the FBI]. . . .

Judge Edgerton held that Dorothy Bailey's dismissal violated both the Constitution and the meager provisional safeguards of the order itself, and he declared:

> Freedoms that may not be abridged by law may not be abridged by executive order.
>
> Appellant's dismissal abridges freedom of speech and assembly . . . [and] freedom of thought. . . .
>
> The government's right to preserve itself in the world as it is has nothing to do with the case. The ominous theory that the right of fair trial ends where defense of security begins is irrelevant.
>
> Whatever her actual thoughts may have been, to oust her as disloyal without trial is to pay too much for protection against any harm that could possibly be done in such a [nonsensitive] job. The cost is too great in morale and efficiency of government workers, in appeal of government employment to independent and inquiring minds, and in public confidence in democracy. But even if such dismissals stengthened the government instead of weakening it, they would still cost too much in constitutional rights.

Judge Edgerton did not prevail. His was the lone dissenting voice in the Court of Appeals. On April 30, 1951, the Supreme Court, deeply divided, rejected his arguments and upheld the legality of the Truman Loyalty Program, of Executive Order 9835, of the Attorney General's list—of the witch-hunts really. The vote of the Justices was 4-4, thus automatically upholding the decision of the Court of Appeals.

These days, I like to think of Judge Edgerton working on his opinion at night on the top floor of the Ontario, in the same study where I began these pages, where my grandfather and I delivered his cleaning.

"We cannot preserve our liberties by sacrificing them," he wrote in the final words of his dissent.

I am trying to remember if his black judicial robes were sent to the little tailor shop to be cleaned and pressed, but in truth, I cannot recall—though this is a book about laundry.

246

Chapter 32

"This order was a pivotal event in the history of this country," my father says again.

"How do you feel about it? Angry?" I ask.

"Yeah, you know, injustices. The cases I lost. What it did to innocent people, you know." There are a lot of pauses in his sentences, and his voice becomes almost inaudible.

I remember the look on his face, the agony, the sadness, the dismay.

"It was a reign of terror."

I have never heard my father talk like that, have never known him to reach for a cliché. But this was no cliché.

Now the words came even more slowly. "You could really say that. It was a reign of terror. You had to live it to know it. But I've seen these people coming into hearings shaking, quivering—because they'd gone to a meeting or really just normally exercised their citizenship rights."

What had caused it finally to end? I asked.

"There weren't enough people," my father said, "they had all been cleaned out. . . . And don't forget there were an awful lot of them."

When had they stopped, these cases? I asked.

"When I left the union, it was '50—it had pretty well reached its peak." Pause.

"By then McCarthy had sort of taken over the stage, because he built on this—and the Un-American Committee."

And sitting across from him at that table, I recognized that element of a boy, naive, an innocent really, asking his father questions about grown-ups, about the world his father knows, trusting and loving and expecting that the answer will be reassuring, even though I know what the answer is going to be, that it won't be all right; but somehow I was still looking for the story to come out okay, with a happy ending. . . . I see it in these lines and I heard it in our voices. And in the look on my father's face as he told me this story:

"I think it had a very serious effect on intellectual life in the country—the kind of applicants you had for federal employment, the kind of people who came to Washington, a real difference from the New Deal. It probably took until the Kennedy administration to begin to recover; there was a whole period of a lack of intellectual pursuit, really until the debate over the Vietnam War." And even then Hoover was still casting his shadow over the government.

I looked away, trying to think of another question.

"Was Eisenhower better on this stuff?"

"I do think his Administration didn't go out for the small fry in the way Truman did—small fry I don't mean in the derogatory sense, I mean the ordinary worker," my father said. Eisenhower had at last faced down McCarthy; by then the Senator was no hero to Americans, the country was finished with him—if not with the larger crusade.

"When you look at all this stuff, with all this behind you, what do you think of it all in terms of your own life—being excluded at a certain point from participating. . . ."

And here his voice broke and became a whisper. "Difficult," he said. "I don't like to think about it."

248

We were talking in half-sentences now—and gestures.

"There's no question in my mind that it's only in recent years that I talk about it at all openly to people. For a while you couldn't even do that, because you'd become unemployable.

"Rarely did I ever mention it to the people I worked with. Even now, only with somebody I'm close to, who knows something about what went on then."

He drew a deep breath. "My approach to things, my approach in the big world—I guess I lost some of my political rights"—and here his voice became unsteady again—"because I never could really ever run for office or participate in a political campaign in the sense of the organized parties, because I'd be subject to so much attention. I would become the issue instead of the candidate. There's some of that."

"Is that what you think you would have wanted to do?"

"I might have done that," he said. "I'm sure I lost the right to do it." The voice was firm again.

"When you went with the union what did you want to do?"

"I was going to stay in the labor movement for the rest of my adult life. It was a conscious decision. I left the government to do that."

For about ten seconds neither of us spoke.

"Was it apparent to you right away that you wouldn't be able to do that at a specific point? When the union was getting thrown out of the CIO, were you thinking about what was going to happen to you?"

"During that period? Well, you fought as long as you realistically could. I quit just a month or two before the union fell apart completely. By '49 we were trying to hold on to our locals. By this time I was occupied fully handling loyalty cases—after the Truman election that's all I did."

"It was clear to you at that point that there was no way you could stay in the labor movement?"

That must have been the worst time of all for him. The CIO had begun its own purge. He must have seen the purpose in his life being drained from him, realized then that he would no longer be a respected member of the community, part of the establishment of the city, of the civilized fraternity. That he would be out of a job, out of his chosen profession forever. He must have known that he would never organize another group of workers. He had become an untouchable. He would be lucky if he could feed his wife and children. He would have seen it all before him then.

"There was no way to carry on," he was saying. "Very few survived. The unions on the left that did survive had enough problems taking care of their own people."

I tried to gather my thoughts. "How did . . . What did . . . You're not like me," I said finally. "I talk a lot about my feelings. What were you feeling?"

"What?"

"What were your feelings? What were you feeling?"

"Well, I'm not that way," he answered.

He looked down at some papers on the table.

"I was feeling ostracized—from society." Pause. "And I was, in a real sense." He played with the papers for a moment. "People stopped seeing us—people with whom I'd had relationships for years called them off. The usual stuff. You really only felt comfortable when you were with people who were in a similar situation."

My mother and father aren't active politically anymore, they hardly keep up with the left—or what's left of it. He reads *The Nation* now, and the *New York Review of Books*. "The *Guardian* became crazy," he explains. "It's dogma. That stuff about 'the system,' about it not making any difference who's President. It's crazy."

I asked, "And today, with the Gellers or Betty Hayes or Dave or . . ."—I was looking for another name—"do you all talk about what happened?"

"We make fun now. About laundries. Laundromats," my father said.

250

Postscript

Once again my father had refused to read the final version of the book, now about to be set in type. He was resigned to the inevitability of its publication, and to the certainty that the book would say my mother and he had been members of the Communist Party; nevertheless, he wanted to register his disapproval in the strongest terms. He pulled from the bookshelf a copy of Jessica Mitford's book and read: "My policy has been to use the real names of Communist [Party members] only with express permission of the individuals so identified in my book."

"That is the decent thing to do," he said. "You didn't afford your mother and me that decency."

My mother asked that I take out the name of the department store. My father insisted that a friend's name be changed, even though the reference was not in the least accusatory. My mother noted that Uncle Morris had tried to help my father find a job in the liquor business, but that the only liquor licenses available at the time in Washington were for stores in black neighborhoods. My father did not want to sell whiskey to impoverished Negroes, and instead he had chosen laundry.

I have come to understand my father's frustration and fear about this book: that having rebuilt his life, he sees this archaeological excavation threatening to dig up not only the shattered bones of a wrecked past but a few loose artifacts that mercifully got buried in the heap the last time around.

Still, I have tried to learn what happened in our family, and to set it down.

In so doing I may or may not have committed an act of disloyalty.

My father and mother never did.

Acknowledgements

In the years since I began work on this book, I have been the beneficiary of the counsel of Joan Didion. Her friendship is one of the joys of my life.

The faith and commitment of Richard Snyder, the chairman of Simon and Schuster, Inc., and of Alice Mayhew, my editor, and of Lynn Nesbit, my agent, have been extraordinary—on this book, as on others. I am deeply grateful for their support and for the special relationship I have enjoyed these many years with S&S.

This project has continually reminded me of how blessed I am in friendships, many of which go back years, some of which are recent. I especially want to note the contributions of those friends who at various stages read the manuscript and offered suggestions and support, among them Alec Baldwin, Philip D. Carter, Richard M. Cohen, Edith Kunhardt Davis, Eve Ensler, Nora Ephron, Joni Evans, Hendrik Hertzberg, Thomas C. Hunter, Jr., Stanley Ikonen, Margaret Jay, Robert G. Kaiser, Shirley MacLaine, Victor Navasky, Magi Nougue-Sans, Philip Roth, David Rieff, John Scanlon, Francoise Schein, and George Stevens, Jr.

For several months, Barbara Feinman assisted me in researching the period I have described, in checking facts and in obtaining historical material. I could not have completed the book without her help and good cheer.

Late in the preparation of the book I benefited from the keen eye of Roslyn Schloss.

At Simon and Schuster, Michael Korda, Tina Jordan, and David Shipley made suggestions, facilitated my requests for all kinds of help and understanding, and became trusted colleagues. Many thanks also to Michele Farinet, George Hodgman, Julia Knickerbocker, Eve Metz, Frank Metz, Vera Schneider, and (again) Sophie Sorkin at S&S.

I also owe special thanks to Elizabeth Taylor, Gordon Brawn, Darlene Grill, Maria Santana, Gladys Seamon, Stan Sitnick, Jack Tynan, and Will Wilson.

Much of this book is based on the recollections of family and friends. Those who shared their knowledge and memories included Joe and Eleanor Belser, Jean Blodgett, Sidney and Estelle Brisker, Clark Clifford, Esther Cohen, Ann Dimond, Robert Donovan, Abe Flaxer, Milton Freeman, Helen Fruchtman, Lillian Hellman, Steve and Gladys Kraft, John

McTernan, Jessica Mitford, Dave and Selma Rein, Al and Nancy Richmond, Rose Rihn, Pat Rihn, Arthur Schlesinger, Jr., Annie Stein, Bob Treuhaft, Doris Walker, and Bob and Evelyn Weinstein.

I cannot adequately express my debt to my grandparents, Thomas and Mary Walker, to my uncle and aunt, Isadore and Rose Taishoff, and to my sisters, Mary Bernstein Hunter and Laura Bernstein Ikonen. Their love is always with me.

And, finally, there are Max and Jacob, who have taught me.

254